Living My Golden Dream

Living My Golden Dream

A SMALL-TOWN CANADIAN GIRL'S AWAKENING IN JAPAN

By Lorna Stuber

No part of this publication may be reproduced, distributed, or transmitted in any form or by any means—including photocopying, recording, or other electronic or mechanical methods—or by any information storage and retrieval system without the prior written permission of the author, except in the case of very brief quotations embodied in critical reviews and certain other non-commercial uses permitted by copyright law.

Cover Design: MiblArt

Interior Layout and Formatting: Lorna Stuber

ISBN: 978-1-7778954-2-6

Copyright ©2022 by Lorna M. Stuber. All rights reserved.

TO AUNTIE DARLENE

Thanks for checking the job ads every week in the summer of 1991 and telling me about a job in Japan that sounded like "it would be a real hoot." It was, and it determined the direction of my life.

I hope you were greeted with a monogrammed, solid-gold fork and a spicy Caesar when you reported to the Pearly Gates.

Thank you for always being supportive and hilarious, and thank you for trusting me with little Duke in his final years.

TABLE OF CONTENTS

FOREWORD

(Written by my giggliest, itsumo genki[1] *student, Masayo, who, after thirty years, is still a good friend of mine!)*

"She is always smiling and her lesson sounds very fun!!! I really want to take her lesson!"

This was my first impression of Lorna at the English school! I didn't know her name at first, but I knew that she must be a very funny person. Then, I asked my teacher what her name was and she told me it was Lorna.

When I first met Lorna, I was fifteen years old, a very shy high school student. I was taking an English lesson with a Japanese teacher because my English was not good enough to take a lesson with a native-speaking teacher. Before the lesson started, I was always waiting on a sofa in front of my classroom. My teacher's classroom was across from Lorna's, so I always heard a lot of laughing voices from her room. When all the students came out of the classroom after the lesson, they all looked very satisfied. Whenever I saw them, I felt that I really want to take her lesson. It was easy for me to picture that her lesson was fun!

---

[1] Itsumo genki: itsumo = always; genki = cheerful, energetic, happy, in good health.

Lorna always said hi to me with a big smile whenever she walked in the hall, but I all I could say back to her was hi because I was too shy and too nervous to speak English at that time. I was worried that I wouldn't be able to understand what she said or she wouldn't understand what I said. I just wished I could speak English better. However, it was a good opportunity for me because I remembered my dream again that I really wanted to be able to speak English fluently and was eager to talk more with Lorna in English. I also realized that I had to change myself. I need to be more outgoing and active in order to be able to improve my English.

The time finally came when I was allowed to move up to a native-speaking teacher's class! My teacher recommended me to take a class with another teacher, but I told my teacher that I really wanted to take Lorna's class. She looked surprised at first, but finally she said okay and arranged a short interview with Lorna.

On the interview day, I was nervous all day, but I realized that it was no problem at all soon after I started talking with Lorna. She greeted and welcomed me with a big smile as usual, and I had so much fun talking with her. I still remember a question she asked me, and I remember my answer well. (Unfortunately, I don't remember what she said, though.) The question was, "What animal would you like to be if you could and why?" I was so relieved that she understood my answer and I passed the interview test! Yes!! From that week, I started taking Lorna's class, which was my first goal!

Soon, I strongly felt that my choice to take Lorna's class was right. Of course, I had lots of fun in class. Through her lessons, I realized how fun speaking English was. I took lessons with Lorna for only six months, but she told me a lot about Canada in class, and I started to think about going abroad. I felt like going to Canada!

When I heard that Lorna was leaving, I was shocked and sad, but going to Canada to visit Lorna became my new goal.

A few months later, she came back to Japan. I was so happy and had an opportunity to invite Lorna to my house. We went to karaoke with my family, and I was surprised how well Lorna could sing a song in Japanese. I sometimes still talk about it with my family. They all remember Lorna's singing, too.

Another two years had passed, and as soon as I started university, I started planning to go on a homestay in Canada. I had wanted to go on a homestay since I met Lorna! I contacted Lorna and she said that she was working at an English school in Calgary. I applied for the school where she worked and visited her! On my first day of the school in Calgary, I was excited to meet her again. Actually, I was too excited to sleep the night before. That day, she came to greet and welcome me with the same smile as she had when she was in Japan. I was very happy.

During my stay in Calgary, my mom visited me. My mom was also very excited to meet Lorna again. My mom remembers that we went to a sushi restaurant together, and one of Lorna's friends put too much soy sauce on his rice! And Lorna also took us to the Stampede. My mom still says that she was impressed with the Stampede and that Lorna is always a kind, polite, and wonderful person.

I still think that Lorna is the best teacher I have ever taken a lesson with. If I hadn't taken her lesson, I wouldn't have become an English teacher. I'm sure that meeting Lorna was a big change for me. I learned from her that speaking English, I mean, having a conversation in English, is so much fun. I believe that English opened a lot of doors for me. Therefore, I wanted to tell a lot of children about it and decided to become an English teacher. I want all of my students to feel "English is fun!" and to have an interest in going abroad. This is my big goal now!

Keeping in touch has become more convenient these days with the Internet, but I enjoy receiving Lorna's handwritten cards. They remind me of the lessons with Lorna writing on the whiteboard!

I can't believe that thirty years have passed since I first met Lorna. I can definitely say that meeting her has made me who I am now!

Since I became an English teacher, I haven't seen Lorna, so I made a plan to visit Canada in 2020, but it was impossible due to COVID. I'd like to meet Lorna, and I need to show off how well I became able to speak English sometime soon. Hopefully, I will go to Canada to meet Lorna in 2022.

—Masayo Shimizu

Mishimi-shi, Shizuoka, Japan

December 2021

A NOTE ON THE LANGUAGE

Spoken Japanese

Japanese is a phonetic language consisting of five vowel sounds as well as *kana*, [2] which are syllables made up of consonant + vowel combinations:

Vowels

- a = pronounced *a* as in *water*
- i = pronounced *ee* as in *meet*
- u = pronounced *oo* as in *food*
- e = pronounced as a short *e* as in *met*
- o = pronounced *o* as in *so*

---

[2] Kana: the two systems of writing Japanese syllables

Samples of consonant-based syllables (kana)

- ka
- ki
- ku
- ke
- ko
- kyo (*Kyo* is one syllable. As an example, compared to the three-syllable English pronunciation of *Tōkyō* [*To-kee-yo*] in Japanese, it's pronounced using two kana for a total of four syllables: Tō-kyō.) More on this in the section below about written Japanese, but a dash over a vowel when writing in Roman characters (*rōma-ji*) indicates that the vowel is pronounced as two syllables. In the case of ō, the accent indicates the second vowel sound is the *u* sound. For example, *Tōkyō* is pronounced as four syllables: *To-u-kyo-u*.
- sa
- shi
- su
- se
- so

Japanese nouns are the same in both singular and plural forms (e g., one kimono, two kimono). In this book, out of respect for the Japanese language, **I have *not* anglicized Japanese words by adding the English -s to form plurals of Japanese nouns.**

Written System

Japanese uses three writing systems:

Kanji are the Chinese characters that are used to represent nouns, adjectives, adverbs, and verbs. These are the same characters that are used in China. So if you can read kanji, you will be able to read in Japan, China, Taiwan, Singapore, and anywhere else that Chinese characters are used. Pronunciation of the kanji differs between the Asian languages, but the meaning represented by kanji is the same across cultures. In Japanese, kanji are interspersed with or preceded by *hiragana* to create the full Japanese word.

Examples of kanji:

金 The base meaning of this kanji (*kin*) is money, but the actual Japanese word for money is *o-kane*, so the hiragana *o* (**お**) is used with the kanji for kin to create the word o-kane: **お金**.

弁当 These two kanji combined mean *bentō* (lunch box). The first kanji, **弁**, means *ben* (valve) and is also used in writing the word for lawyer (**弁護士** [*bengoshi*]). Additionally, adding the kanji for seller **屋** (*ya*) to bentō means *bentō-ya* (or bentō seller **弁当屋**). Even if you cannot speak Japanese (or Chinese, Taiwanese, etc.), knowing how to read kanji will enable you to read in these languages since the meaning of the kanji is the same. For example, being able to read bentō-ya **弁当屋**, meaning lunch box seller, will help visitors find sustenance in any Asian country that uses kanji regardless of the pronunciation of these characters! Survival skills!

Kana

1. Hiragana (a type of kana) is cursive. It is used for parts of speech such as articles, possessives, and prepositions.

Vowels in hiragana

- あ = a pronounced *a* as in *water*
- い = i pronounced *ee* as in *meet*
- う = u pronounced *oo* as in *food*
- え = e pronounced as a short *e* as in *met*
- お = o pronounced *o* as in *so*

A sample of consonant-based syllables in hiragana

- か = ka
- き = ki
- く = ku
- け = ke
- こ = ko
- きょ = kyo (even though it is pronounced as a single syllable, *kyo* is written by using the kana for *ki* き and a subscript of the kana for *yo* よ)
- さ = sa
- し = shi
- す= su

- せ = se
- そ = so

2. *Katakana* is similar to hiragana but more angular, and it is used for words from other languages that are used in Japanese written text. For example, my name, *Lorna,* is linguistically challenging in Japanese since there is no L in the language. The closest consonant sound is R. My name would be written and pronounced with three syllables, either as *Ro-ru-na* (ロルナ) or *Ro-o-na* (ローナ). When writing katakana, long vowels (vowels that are pronounced as two syllables) are expressed using an en dash (–). So in the second example, instead of using the katakana symbol for *o* for the second syllable in my name, it is spelled with *ro*, followed by an en dash to indicate a second *o* syllable, and then the kana for *na*. The second option, ローナ, quickly became my preferred way of writing my name when I was in Japan.

Vowels in katakana

- ア = a pronounced *a* as in *water*
- イ = i pronounced *ee* as in *meet*
- ウ = u pronounced *oo* as in *food*
- エ = e pronounced as a short *e* as in *met*
- オ = o pronounced *o* as in *so*

A sample of consonant-based syllables in katakana

- カ = ka
- キ = ki
- ク = ku
- ケ = ke
- コ = ko
- キョ = kyo (even though it is pronounced as a single syllable, *kyo* is written by using the kana for *ki* キ and a subscript of the kana for *yo* ヨ)
- サ = sa
- シ = shi
- ス = su
- セ = se
- ソ = so

Rōma-ji (Roman characters or "the English alphabet") are being used more and more in Japan. The West has had increasing influence on Japanese culture, particularly through movies and music, as has globalization in general. As such, using the Roman alphabet for some words and phrases has become not only trendy but also beneficial for businesses.

Japanese Names

As is the custom in many Asian cultures, adults in Japan are referred to by their last names.

The honorifics used for adults are *-san* (Mr., Mrs., or Ms.) or *-sensei* (teacher, master). For children, *-kun* (boys) and *-chan* (girls) are used.

For example, a teacher named *Kyoko Tanaka* would be called *Tanaka-sensei.* A businessperson named *Nao Suzuki* would be called *Suzuki-san.*

Children are often referred to by their first names along with the honorific, so a girl named *Yukiko Nakamura* would be called *Yukiko-chan* or, more commonly *Yuki-chan.* (When talking or referring to children, names are often shorted into nicknames.) A boy named *Shuji Kumamoto* would be called *Shuji-kun.*

First names that end in -ko are almost always female names: *Tomoko*, *Keiko*, *Naoko*, *Yoshiko*, etc.

Because I taught English, and because language and culture cannot be separated, I always referred to my students by their first names without honorifics—except in the case of older gentlemen. If my students were businessmen and were older than I was, I wanted to be respectful, as I would in my own culture. Therefore, I called my older male students by their last name and either -san or -sensei, depending on their standing in society.

My students and Japanese co-workers referred to me as *Lorna-sensei,* thus embracing the Canadian custom to call me by my first name—but also ensuring to include the respectful sensei since I was a teacher.

INTRODUCTION

There's a Big World Out There

I grew up on a cattle ranch located a ten-minute drive from a town of 3,000 people. We were a two-hour drive from the closest major city, Calgary, Alberta. On average, my parents, sister, and I only ventured into the big city twice each year: to shop for new school clothes in August and for Christmas shopping in the fall.

When I moved away from home at seventeen to attend university, I took with me a naïveté that has stayed with me to a certain extent even now, decades later. I've always been one to keep my eyes wide open, seeking knowledge and skills and taking on new adventures. I'm naturally inquisitive, open-minded, and eager to learn. At times, my hunger for knowledge of history and culture, in particular, can be voracious. Culture has always been a huge interest of mine, possibly stemming from the fact that for the first ten years of my life, I had a fascinating great-grandfather who didn't speak English. My sister, cousins, and I were, in fact, the first generation in my family to speak English as a first language even though my great-grandparents all immigrated to Canada more than fifty years before I was born. I grew up hearing stories like the instance of my dad running home at noon on his first day of school because he didn't understand what his teachers were saying. I also watched my grandmother translate between my great-grandpa and my mom. By the time she grew up, Mom had lost her first language—German. I remember sitting at my great-grandpa's feet, my eyes fixed on this wrinkly old man who I couldn't speak to without my grandmother as a translator, wishing I could ask him to tell me the stories of the land where he grew up—where and how he spent the first eighteen years of his life before crossing the Atlantic. Wondering about and imagining his younger life in an area that is now part of Romania was my first mental excursion to another country.

When I was around eight years old, my Sunday school teacher gave us homework—to write a letter to a missionary. Little did I know that letter was the seed of what became the entire tree of my life. The missionary I chose as my recipient was working in Haiti at the time. During the next twenty years, while we continued to write to each other, she moved between Haiti, Colombia, and South Korea. I met her a few times over those years when she came back to Canada to share her stories with the churches that were supporting her. Hearing about her work in vastly different cultures sparked a dream within me of becoming a teacher and someday teaching in another country.

Around the time I started writing to this missionary and envisioning her experiences, my elementary school teacher brought a bundle of little orange-and-white forms to class one day and asked who would like a pen pal in another country. As shy as I was to ever raise my hand to answer questions or take part in class discussions, I immediately shot my hand into the air, and my teacher gave me one of the forms. Over the next few years, I continued to fill out these forms, requesting more and more friends in other countries as I devotedly wrote to the pen pals I had already acquired. By the time the forms stopped coming, I had made friends in Italy, Germany, Finland, Egypt,

South Korea, and Australia. All of them wrote to me in English, and all but the Australian were learning English as their second or third language. These friendships served as my introduction to communicating with someone who was trying to learn my mother tongue.

I continued to dream about teaching abroad, but as a teenager, I didn't fully conceptualize what that would look like. I figured I would need to become a missionary, and whatever I ended up teaching and wherever I would go would just fall into place. By the time I entered university, I had matured and come to terms with the fact that teaching abroad was an exotic dream that happens only to other people. I was just a lowly farm girl from the Canadian prairies, and to live abroad was something that seemed out of reach. And I was re-evaluating my religious beliefs to the point where I was beginning to question whether missionaries did a disservice by overriding culture instead of respecting and preserving it. I resigned myself to becoming a high school English teacher, aiming to inspire teenagers to love Shakespeare as much as I did when I was in high school.

But no, the dream that had planted itself in my eight-year-old brain had its own path for me already set out, and teaching abroad is exactly what I ended up doing. The dream that had been incubating for more than ten years started to churn itself toward the surface of my life.

Go West, Young Woman

The summer after I graduated from university with my teaching degree, I was working at my church camp in southwestern Alberta, near the Montana border. The camp was smack-dab in the heart of the Rockies and a fifteen-minute drive from the nearest town.

This was before the days of cellphones, but I was reachable by phone if anyone called the camp number. My aunt Darlene had appointed herself as my job hunter since I couldn't actively look for teaching jobs from such a remote location. Every Saturday, she flipped through the job section of the *Calgary Herald* and called me with any ads that she thought might interest me. There were two in particular that piqued my interest.

I applied for a one-year position in a small southern Alberta town teaching grade 4 language arts and music while the permanent teacher was on maternity leave. On paper, this seemed like the ideal teaching position for me with my background in and passion for music and language. And grade 4 had been my favourite age when I was student teaching. The principal of the school interviewed me and one other applicant, and during my interview, I felt that he showed his hand when he asked me if this was my first interview for a teaching job. I said it was. He replied by assuring me I was doing well, which I interpreted in the moment as, "Don't worry. Even though I'm not going to hire you, you have good interview skills." My gut told me that's what he meant, and sure enough, he hired the other candidate.

I wasn't heartbroken because, truth be told, I had applied for that job out of a sense of obligation. I had just finished a bachelor's degree in education. In each of my student teaching rounds, I had purposely requested placements at grade 1, upper-elementary, junior high, and senior high schools so that I could gauge which age group I felt best suited for. The grade 4–5 age group was my favourite.

But I had lost my drive to be a schoolteacher. In fact, after several significant life events and family traumas that had nothing to do with my education, I withdrew from my third year of university with only five days left, slamming my education to a halt. I spent the summer re-evaluating my life plan. After hundreds of hours of self-exploration and discussions with one of my supervising professors, I realized that being a schoolteacher was not for me after all and that I needed to determine what I would do instead. Rather than switch programs, I decided to finish my education degree, having convinced myself that it's a good degree to have and that it would open up more doors besides simply teaching in a traditional school. And an education degree would also open up more doors than a bachelor's degree in English would, so I forged on and graduated in the summer of 1991.

The only other job I applied for that summer was the one that I took. My aunt called me on another Saturday in late July telling me about the teaching jobs posted in that week's *Calgary Herald*. Nope, nope, nope, nope. I was starting to think I was going to be unemployed for a while after my summer camp gig ended.

Then, before we ended the phone call, she had something different to offer.

"Here's one. I think this one sounds like a hoot!"

She proceeded to read to me a job ad looking for teachers to move to Japan for two years and teach English. The job wasn't for a school system posting; it was for a private language school, which Japan and other Asian countries were flooded with, and the school had a hiring office in Vancouver. I was to send my application to that office, and then, if selected, head there for the interview.

Japan! I knew almost nothing about Japan, and it seemed so far away from the Canadian prairies. But that childhood dream of teaching in another country for a few years suddenly started to come back into focus. I immediately shrugged and thought, *There's no way they would hire little ol' me for something so exotic and exciting. I'm just an ordinary person with nothing extraordinary to offer*. But I also thought I had nothing to lose by applying. *And when they reject me*, I thought, *I can at least say I tried to make this dream come true.*

Only a couple of weeks after I mailed off my application, I took several days off work to drive to Vancouver for the job interview. I gave strict instructions to my boss that, if my mother were to phone, he was not to tell her where I was going but to tell her I would call her in a few days. I didn't want her freaking out about the possibility of me moving to Asia for two years when I had no idea whether I had even the slightest chance at this job.

I couldn't afford to fly, and so off I went, headed west in my clunky Dodge Neon that I was PRETTY sure would get me to the West Coast. I picked up a friend along the way in eastern BC, and when we arrived at the coast, I dropped him off at the Tsawwassen ferry station so he could head to Vancouver Island. I would join him and some other friends from university there after I was done my job interview. My home for the next couple of nights was the hostel at Jericho Beach because I was too broke for a real hotel room. I settled in to prepare for a job interview that was almost as foreign as the land I would potentially be going to.

The interview office was in downtown Vancouver, and as a naive twenty-one-year-old prairie girl, being downtown alone in such a big city was daunting. As my mother had dutifully taught me, I headed there early enough that I gave myself lots of time to find the office building. At that point in life, I had barely even been to downtown Calgary, so the high buildings of downtown Vancouver were overwhelming; I really was in THE BIG CITY. Tilting my neck up to admire the tall glass structures surrounding me was a great prelude to what was in store for my life over the next few years.

I found the office building and reported for my interview. It went well. It was pretty standard, with two people interviewing me and asking the typical questions about my experience and reasons for applying. I emphasized to them that since I was a child, my only life goal had been to get my teaching degree and then teach abroad for a few years. I assured them that I was definitely open to staying longer than the initial two-year commitment. I shared that I was looking at this as not only an opportunity to work abroad but to travel and learn about other cultures. I left their office with a sense of certainty—completely the opposite of how I had felt after the grade 4 teaching job interview. My gut told me I had a great shot at getting hired, but I fought back the urge to get too set on the job in case they didn't choose me. Because this was before the days of cellphones and I was an out-of-towner, their process was for me to call them at the end of the day to be told whether I had passed this initial interview or not. If I passed, there would be two more days of "interviews"—which were more like training—starting the next morning. If I was not selected, I was done with the interview process.

That night, alone in a city where I knew no one and had no money, I spent the evening at the beach a few steps away from the hostel. Before heading to the beach, I had called my interviewers, and sure enough, I had passed the initial interview—but the job was not yet mine. I was scheduled for two days of training interviews, for which they were going to pay me a small stipend. Then they would make their hiring decisions. The reality of the process I had entered into started to sink in. We were past the "Aw, heck, I'll throw my application at this just for kicks" stage, and people were seriously considering me for a job teaching halfway around the planet.

As I sat on the dock looking westward, I knew in my gut that I was going to be headed to Japan for two years. Maybe more.

Looking out at the black water under the night sky, with the reflections of lights from the dock and the bright moon bouncing off the water, I realized that I was sitting at a crossroads. Behind me lay my whole country of Canada (except Vancouver Island, which was "out there" in front of me). But ahead, WAAAAYYYY off into the Pacific Ocean, was Japan—a country I had never even thought about visiting, much less living in, but one that nevertheless was gently pulling me toward it. I knew I would be going there. I was a little afraid of the unknown, but I also felt a great sense of peace that the dream eight-year-old me had hatched was actually coming true. I had no concept at all of what my future held, but I knew that moving farther west from that dock was what I needed to do.

I don't know how long I sat there, but it was as long as I needed to in order to accept the impact of the can of worms I had just opened up. I knew I would be offered this job. I knew I would say yes, and I knew that taking this job was a huge step. Up to that point, I had led a pretty sheltered life. Even though living and teaching abroad had been my main dream in life, it had also been only that—a dream. Something unreachable, something exotic, something that happened to other people—not me, the naive, unassuming, young farm girl who had held on to a dream, never fully realizing that the dream was achievable.

I've always had big dreams, and in the past thirty years, I've made a point to achieve many of them. At that moment, though, I was a twenty-one-year-old whose first grandiose dream was within reach. I knew there was a huge world out there, and although I had always yearned to bite into it, the reality of my dreams materializing was a little nerve-wracking. Committing to two years in Asia, accompanied only by my suitcases, would be quite different from going on a six-week adventure with twenty-eight other Canadian and American youth to the jungles of Peru. I had done so the summer after my first year of university, and it had been the only other time I had left North America. As I sat on that dock on Jericho Beach, my mindset became solemn. I wasn't yet excited about the future ahead of me. I was in the stunned, *What have I done?* phase. The realization of the phrase, "Be careful what you wish for—you just might get it" started to sink in.

This was really going to happen.

Despite my worries, the next two days were an awful lot of fun. The hiring office had called in a few of us to do training together. The training included each candidate teaching some mock lessons and the interviewers introducing us to company policy and the school's structured teaching methodology. During the training, I felt as though the decision had been already made—that I was being trained for a job I had already been offered and accepted, although that step had not yet occurred. The atmosphere was businesslike yet comfortable, and as the two days progressed, I felt more and more sure that this was the entry point to the next phase of my life. The company and the work they were hiring for felt like a great fit, and I had the strong sense that they would choose me. I knew that I had already chosen them.

The initial interview had been on a Wednesday, immediately followed by the two days of training. By the end of the Friday, I was finished with business and crossed over to Vancouver Island to join my friends for a mini vacation before heading back to Alberta. After a bit of frolicking for half a day, my friend and I headed back east.

On the ferry from Victoria to Tsawwassen that Saturday, I called my mom from the pay phone on the ferry. She wasn't happy. She had indeed called the camp while I was away and was not impressed when my boss wouldn't tell her where I was—only that I would call her on the weekend. By this time, I was sure I would be accepting a job, thereby committing at least two years of my life to living in Japan. Even so, I only told her about the interview and that the hiring office would be calling me Monday morning with their decision. I informed her that I was currently on the ferry back to the mainland, that everything was fine, and that I hadn't wanted to get her worked up in case this job interview went nowhere. That day was also her birthday, so I wished her a happy birthday as we ended the somewhat tense phone call.

I arrived back in Alberta Sunday night and reported for work the next morning. I had to remind myself that Vancouver was one hour behind us, so when 10 a.m. rolled around and the phone hadn't rung yet, I assured myself that was not necessarily a bad sign—that the recruiters were likely just getting their morning coffee and settling into their desks.

The phone rang at 10:20, and within a few minutes, I had given away the next two years of my life.

The next phone call, which I made to my mother, was more nerve-wracking than the one I had just received.

"Hi, Mom. It's me."

"So?"

"So, they just phoned me. They offered me the job and I took it. But I won't be going for a while. I have to wait till my work visa comes through, and they said that will take at least three months."

"I knew it. I told your dad at breakfast this morning, 'She's going to get the job. She's going to Japan, you know.'"

I knew this was going to create a lot of ripples in my family. For the past twenty-one years, the entire time I had been on Earth, everyone on my mom's side of my family—cousins, aunts, uncles, grandparents—had been together for every Christmas, Easter, and Thanksgiving, even those who lived at least two hours away. I was about to become the one to break that tradition. My going to university a three-hour drive away hadn't broken the Christmas tradition, but obviously, Japan was not within driving distance. Our whole family's dynamic was about to change because of this decision I had made.

"Well, anyway, I told you I would call and tell you when I heard from them, so that's what's happened. I will talk to you later."

Click.

Gulp.

CHAPTER 1

ARRIVAL

Leaving on a Jet Plane

March 3, 1992. As my plane touched down at Narita International Airport outside of Tōkyō, I reflected on the previous fourteen hours.

After waiting six months for my work visa, I stood in front of the check-in agent in the Calgary airport. She told me that to enter Japan (and in fact, to board the first flight in my itinerary—Calgary to Vancouver), I needed a return ticket as proof that I would be coming back to Canada. I didn't have that proof. What I had was a paper copy of my two-year contract, but I had no idea when I would be coming back to Canada, even for a visit. Money was tight, so I had bought a one-way ticket instead of an open round-trip ticket. I had told all of my friends and family to not expect to see me for at least a year. I only had ten vacation days per year of my contract, and I had every intention of using those ten days to explore as much of Asia as I could while I was living there.

At long last, my contract was enough proof to convince the ticket agent to allow me to proceed, but she relented only after a good amount of coaxing. As I passed through security, I remained a little nervous at having been informed I needed proof that I was *eventually* coming back. Until we were actually in the air, I had visions of being escorted off the plane before leaving Alberta. Not so, thankfully.

My plane made the short hop over the Rockies from Calgary to Vancouver, where Colleen, a young woman I had done my teaching degree with, met me during my layover for a lunch visit. This vivacious and funny friend of mine had the distinct honour of being the last familiar face to see and talk to me before I left Canadian soil. I didn't know when I would return, nor did I have the slightest clue what lay ahead of me for the two years of my life that I had committed to the experience. I was a little nervous, but Colleen distracted me from all of that simply by being the fun friend that she was. We spent a couple of hours laughing and eating fresh seafood. She was a great coach, giving me ideas of what to do on the long flight ahead. "This is the beginning of a huge step in your life," she said. "While you're on the plane, make a list of fifty other things you want to do in life before you die!" was her suggestion. (This was long before anyone used the phrase *bucket list*.)

Great advice. I love lists. As I settled into the long flight, I pulled out the notebook I had brought with me. (I never go anywhere without one!) Several hours into the flight, I wrote out that list of fifty life goals that Colleen had encouraged me to compile. They were HARD to come up with, even at age twenty-two when I had so much life ahead of me. I wrote out the typical goals: own a house one day, travel to ________ (insert names of various countries, cities, and archaeological sites), write a book.

I also journaled my thoughts about what I was doing—where I was going literally and figuratively. I was at the clichéd crossroads of life: a newly graduated teacher taking on her first professional job, but not in another town or province. No, I had to go to the other side of the world, to a country I didn't know much about, where I knew no one, and where I would have only a rudimentary understanding of the language. I couldn't have been entering a more foreign experience if I had been going to the moon.

And I was alone ... which was fine ... but also scary. As an independent, strong-willed, adventurous type, I have never shied away from jumping solo into something that many others may be more hesitant to dip a toe into. But I truly WAS naive sitting on that plane. So I wrote about all the people I had just said goodbye to, all the events that had led to me sitting on that plane. And I wept. I wasn't sad or upset or even scared, but overwhelmed. I was sitting on a large machine that was taking me to the place where my lifelong dream would come true. I was really doing it.

I'm Here, Japan!

At Narita, Tōkyō's international airport, I was disappointed (and surprised—that naïveté kicked in again) to discover that the customs officer spoke fluent English. Hmph. As our plane landed, I had hauled out my pocket-sized travel dictionary for nothing.

When the customs officer saw me coming with a huge duffle bag, a backpack, a garment bag, a guitar, and a briefcase, I got a sinking feeling from the look on his face. Maybe THIS was where I would be sent back.

"Why so many bags?" he asked.

"Because I'm going to be living here for two years," I replied cautiously. "I'm an English teacher."

"Have a nice stay," was his reply.

That was it?

That was it. I was in Japan, free and clear.

The next challenge was finding Naoko, the manager of my school, who was scheduled to meet me at Narita and bring me to the city I would be living in.

"How hard can it be?" I thought to myself. After all, the school had been sent a picture of me. Surely, she would be able to pick me out of the crowd.

No one was waiting for me with a sign. Or without a sign. Scouring the crowd, I realized it was futile for me to try and find her; I had no idea what she looked like and there were SO many people scurrying about in this busy airport. She could be any of them. (Well, any of the women!) I settled into waiting until she recognized me, and I figured the best course of action was to wait in one place. This was partly because I had a truckload of luggage, but also so we wouldn't be wandering in circles, missing each other.

Waiting.

Waiting.

Waiting.

Waiting ...

After half an hour of studying the faces of the swarms of people coming and going, I came to the conclusion that my contract was a hoax.

There is no job. There is no company. Since July, this has all been a conspiracy—a joke played by my auntie who had seen the job ad in the Calgary Herald. *A joke played by my friends back home who had obviously hired Marnie and Nao (the two recruiters at the alleged hiring office in Vancouver). Someone I knew must have also found a way to intercept my passport when I sent it to the consulate in Edmonton because surely my work visa is a fake, too. And clearly, they somehow planted the fluent customs official who let me through. This was all a big conspiracy to see if I was actually delusional enough to just pack up and move halfway across the world to a country I know little about without having done any research into the country or the company that was supposedly hiring me. OK, guys, joke's over—I AM that ridiculous, and I AM desperate enough to fulfill my lifelong dream that I would just sign a contract and go.*

I started looking at the departure board to see when the next flight to Vancouver was. No one was there to meet me; I had no idea how to get where I was supposed to go. I had no idea even WHERE I was supposed to go. A city called Fujisawa, which was somewhere on the outskirts of Tōkyō. That's all I knew. There was nothing I could do but return home.

I looked up at the departure board again and started thinking how I was going to undo this silly decision that had taken over the previous six months of my life. I had spent three months working as a waitress to get a bit of income before coming to Japan. I had spent $1,000 on a new wardrobe because this school in Japan would only allow female teachers to wear dresses and skirts, and as a fresh university grad, I didn't have many dress clothes. I had squeezed money out of my bank account to buy my one-way ticket, and I was going to be living on pennies until that first paycheque came at the end of March. It was becoming obvious that that paycheque did not exist. I could pay for a return trip ticket with the cash I had brought with me, but I would be returning home with no plan, no car, no more money, no job prospects. The past six months had all been about getting ready for this step: introductory language lessons, selling my car to my parents, arranging for my mom to make my student loan payments at the bank with the money I would send her from Japan, cancelling my Alberta health insurance, and so on. A sense of defeat and utter disappointment started to settle in.

"Ro-o-na-san?"[3]

I turned around. A smiling Japanese woman introduced herself as Naoko and apologized for being late.

The adventure was about to begin.

Squishy Fishy

I was surprised that I needed to report to work the day after landing in Japan. In my mind, giving new arrivals at least a day to adjust to the time change would have made sense, but my company was sponsoring my work visa and paying for my hotel, so I was on the clock from day one. It made sense that they put me to work immediately.

Naoko picked me up at the hotel on my first morning in Fujisawa, the city that was to be home for at least the next two years. I dutifully followed her to the school, dressed in my navy blue skirt and jacket and toting my brand-new briefcase. I had done enough research to know that in the Japanese workplace, employees were expected to dress well and appear professional. No casual Fridays here!

[3] -San: the honorific used to address people by their last name. It is used for both men and women and is therefore equivalent to Mr., Mrs., and Ms.

When we arrived at the school, I was introduced to the staff members. Nine Japanese women on staff taught English to the beginner students. Our school had three foreign teachers who were assigned students of a high-beginner level and up. Penny was from Ontario; Ken was from Montana; and Michelle, the teacher I was replacing, was from Philadelphia. Some of the Japanese teachers on staff worked part-time and wouldn't arrive until later in the day.

Once Naoko had given me a quick tour, she left me with Michelle. My first three days were Michelle's last three days. I joined her classes and observed while she introduced me to her students, who were about to become my students, and did a bit of training with me. She also showed me around the area near the school a little during our lunch break.

There were scads of restaurants near our school since it was near the city's main train station: KFC, McDonald's, Japanese burger chains, and restaurants offering every kind of Japanese food imaginable. After we enjoyed a Japanese lunch, I assumed we would be going back to the school, but Michelle then guided me to some of the shops in the area. She was finishing her contract with the school, but she had already married a Japanese man and was planning her move to the next city on the train line from Fujisawa to begin her new life. So instead of heading back after our lunch hour was up, she pulled me into some stores where she proceeded to leisurely shop for her new home.

I pointed out to her that we had already been gone for more than an hour and perhaps we should be getting back? She assured me that it was no problem to be out of the school longer than an hour since her teaching schedule had a lengthy break at that time. And she quipped back at me, "Besides, what are they going to do … fire me?" and laughed heartily. I laughed along with her, but I wasn't convinced that taking an extended lunch break on my first day at work reflected well on me.

We returned in plenty of time for the next class and faced no reprimand whatsoever.

The workday was from noon until 9 p.m. All teachers' evenings were crammed with lessons because that's when businessmen, college students, and high school students were free from their daytime commitments to take language classes. The school had an energizing buzz that evening. All of the teachers' students were excited that a new Canadian teacher had arrived.

After all classes had ended, my new co-worker Ken invited me to join a group of his students going out for drinks and snacks.

"You should go!" Michelle nudged me.

My first dilemma in a new country: I was interested in going, and I also knew that Japan was The Land of Ultimate Politeness, meaning I really should accept the invitation so as to not appear ungrateful. I was, however, utterly exhausted mentally and physically because of jet lag and already being overwhelmed with all I was beginning to absorb about this starkly different culture. But I wanted to start connecting with people, so I accepted.

The night didn't go on terribly long, but as the new arrival, I was definitely the center of attention, which put even more pressure on me to keep my eyelids open and remain energetic and cheerful. Ken's students were exceptionally hospitable to me, obviously eager to welcome me to their country and start introducing their culture to me. I sampled every kind of food and drink that was ordered for me, fearful of offending anyone. The students had asked me what I liked. I admitted that I had had little exposure to Japanese food prior to arriving but was open to trying anything they recommended. Nothing they ordered for me was too out of the ordinary. They choose a great selection of typical Japanese foods, and we all stuck to drinking beer.

"You must try sushi," one of the students insisted.

I had never tried sushi up to that point. I knew it was pretty standard fare in Japan, and I was a little nervous at the thought of trying raw fish for the first time. Still, I didn't want to turn my nose up at anything and appear picky or ungrateful.

The students showed me how to pick it up with my chopsticks and pop it into my mouth in its entirety. The slippery tuna hit the roof of my mouth. I blinked. It was so … cold … and soft … and squishy … and … uncooked … and … slippery. The taste was unique but not unappealing. The texture, however, was unnerving. I didn't know if I could ever get used to eating something this slithery.

"What do you think?"

I was on the hot seat.

"It's delicious!" I lied. They beamed, pleased that they had properly welcomed me.

I began to think to myself, *This might be a long two years. Thank goodness for the KFC across the street from my school!*

Wakarimasen! [4]

My sense of direction has always been strong. I'm good at finding my way around unfamiliar cities and towns, and I don't need to use the sun to know in which direction I am heading when hiking

---

[4] Wakarimasen: I don't understand.

in the mountains. Japan, for some reason, stole all of that away from me. Maybe it's as simple as the fact that the streets in Japan's cities and towns are not on a grid like they are in Canada and the US. Instead, the roads curve and swerve, and it doesn't help that there are no street signs. The buildings, while not terribly high, are so close together in places that it's hard to see the sun—which is ironic, seeing as Japan is the "land of the rising sun."

After we took the three-hour train ride from Narita to Fujisawa on the day I had arrived, Naoko had guided me to my hotel, then to my school briefly, and then back to the hotel. There I settled in for my first night sleeping in my new land. From my teeny tiny hotel room, I made a quick call to my mom. (The call itself was quick; trying to figure out how to make an international call wasn't.) I assured her I had arrived intact and then went to bed.

Naoko had met me the next morning to bring me to the school for my first official day but left me alone to find my way after that. After the evening out with Ken and his students at the end of my first day in Japan, I relied heavily on my usually accurate sense of direction to get myself back to my hotel.

The *izakaya*[5] we had gone to after work was close to the school. I decided the most surefire way to find my hotel would be to quickly head back to the school and backtrack my way to the hotel, retracing my steps from the morning. I had no trouble finding the school. Getting there from the hotel that morning had been easy, so I thought

---

[5] Izakaya: an informal Japanese pub-style establishment. Izakaya are popular for after-work get-togethers with co-workers or for business people to entertain clients.

I was being clever. Should be easy to get back to the hotel, *ne?*[6] I walked from the school to the river, which I distinctly remembered from the morning trek. I knew my hotel was tucked away on a side street near the river. I knew I had to turn when I got to the 7-Eleven just before the bridge, so I turned onto a path. It started to rain. And I didn't have an umbrella.

I walked for about three blocks until I realized that I was not headed in the right direction. Looking ahead, I saw that there were no more streets turning off the path I was on for about as far as I could see. I turned back.

It started to pour.

日本

As a prairie girl, born and raised on a farm in central Alberta, I had been brainwashed to hope and pray for rain in the summer; the crops always needed it. During my first twenty-two years, my family and I always celebrated rain, and although we had heard of those gadgets called *umbrellas* that people in movies and cities used, I had never even held one in my hand. On that first night in Japan, I was on the cusp of learning that an umbrella would be one of my most prized possessions during my stay.

日本

I could see the 7-Eleven in the distance. Knowing that my hotel was somewhere between me and that store, I turned down a street

[6] Ne: isn't it?/don't you think? (Or, as we Canadians say, "eh?") When you say ne, you must quickly tilt your head slightly, dropping your ear about one-third of the way to your shoulder.

before reaching the convenience store. I used the same logic I would use at home: since the streets there run parallel to each other, even if I were on the wrong street here, I would eventually find my hotel by zigzagging my way through the city streets.

However, the streets in Japan are not parallel to each other. Canadian logic did not apply in this situation, which I would realize as the evening wore on.

It continued to pour, and I still didn't have an umbrella. I could see the lighted sign of the Ocean Terrace Hotel a few blocks away, which was NOT my hotel and which I didn't remember seeing that morning.

I turned down a different street, stubbornly holding onto my Canadian logic. I searched for something—anything—that looked familiar, but nope. Nuthin. The only familiar landmark I eventually saw was a Denny's, so I headed there to try and get my bearings. Then I had four choices, but I couldn't remember where my accommodation (the Fujisawa Hotel) was in relation to the Denny's.

Wet, tired, cold, frustrated, and illiterate, I stopped at a gas station to ask for directions but was unsuccessful in getting anyone to talk with me. I wasn't being assertive enough, and the person working there also seemed to be avoiding me. We were probably equally terrified of trying to speak to the other. I once again ventured out to face the elements and hopefully stumble upon my elusive hotel.

By this time, I was starting to have flashbacks of my airport experience from the day before when I was stranded and helpless. I was beginning to think my only option was to go back to the school, sleep in the doorway, and report to work the next day wet, bedraggled, and wearing the same clothes I was currently wearing. The last factor would have been entirely acceptable since wearing uniforms was common in the workplace. However, it would have been clear that I had not only slept in my clothes but that I had been out in the rain in them, too—which would have been entirely *unacceptable*. Not to mention embarrassing, and I certainly didn't want to embarrass myself in this, my new home.

After an hour of wandering, the magical hour of midnight struck, and I finally summoned up the courage to saunter into the Ocean Terrace Hotel (which I had NO trouble finding, over and over and over) to ask about their competition. After walking past the Ocean Terrace no fewer than three times, I decided my innate stubbornness and fear of speaking to strangers, especially in this foreign land, weren't doing me any favours. I entered.

My hope was that if no one spoke any English, I could at least make myself understood somehow by getting across the message that I was looking for the Fujisawa Hotel. I reckoned that if nothing else, writing the name of the hotel on a piece of paper with a question mark behind it and wildly gesturing to the street outside with a confused look on my face would get said message across.

The front desk clerk spoke enough English to understand that I was lost and was kind enough to draw me a map clearly showing me where the Fujisawa Hotel was. I thanked him immensely, made my way back to the 7-Eleven, turned, walked one more block down what was surely the *only* street I hadn't been down three times that evening, and found my bed.

Japanese People Are Kind and Generous, and So Is NTT[7]

Two mornings later, I checked out of my hotel and was on my way to real life. I would be moving into my apartment that night after work. The great debate for the previous two days, however, was what to do with all of my luggage during the day. I had to report to work from the hotel, but there was no way I could carry all of my luggage to the school with me.

My dilemma was quickly solved when I hauled my language guide out of my pocket and found the page with, "Can I keep my luggage here?" on it. The hotel staff was courteous and helpful while checking two of my bags into storage. My duffle bag had already been delivered to the school, and I could carry my guitar and briefcase to school with me that morning since both were light.

While the clerk was punching my information into the computer to check me out of my room, I flipped to another page in my language guide and proudly asked, "How much are my telephone charges?" My mom and I had only talked for a couple of minutes on that first night since I was tired. Still, I was sure the phone charges for an international call from a hotel room would be ridiculously high, so at checkout, I wanted to make sure that I covered the cost of the call. My school was paying for my hotel, but it seemed only fair not to stiff them for what I anticipated would be anywhere between a C$20–$50 phone call. The clerk handed me a receipt showing I owed a total of ¥3 (equal to about four Canadian cents). Immediately, I began to try and explain that I had called Canada and that my bill must surely be much higher. The language barrier presented a problem and the clerk got

[7] NTT: Nippon Telegraph and Telephone, Japan's national telecommunications company

confused and flustered. I had also embarrassed him by pointing out that he had made a mistake. Four more people came out of a backroom to help him.

Ten minutes later, after much hubbub and back and forth with five people trying to help me, I was handed a new receipt by the smiling clerk who had corrected his mistake. The new total: ¥10 (about twelve cents). I paid it and left.

Fancy Meeting You Here!

I've never felt so alone as I did during the first year I lived in Japan. I visited Tōkyō for day trips now and then on my days off. Walking down its dense streets, surrounded by millions of people but being visibly different from most of them in a homogenous society and not being able to speak their language is ironically deeply isolating. Don't get me wrong. My three-year stint in Japan was an incredible experience. Moving there was one of the best decisions of my life, and I love what those three years gave me. But it was also *really* hard at times. I missed my family. I missed the Rocky Mountains. I missed the big, blue Alberta sky. And I missed Caesar salad.

A married couple I knew from my university days was living in Ōsaka with their two young children at the same time I was settling into my time in Japan. They had arrived in Ōsaka to work not long before I arrived in the Tōkyō suburbs. I lived forty-five minutes outside of Tōkyō and wanted to see both Ōsaka and Kyōto, a three-hour train ride from where I lived, so I planned a short trip to that area for a few days about six months into my stay. I arranged to meet up with these friends for a day.

Their boys were both under five at the time, so the best lunch spot for them halfway through touring around Ōsaka for the day was McDonald's. We had our McFood, and as we were McLeaving, the mother needed to take a few minutes to strap the boys into their strollers. I was standing a few steps outside the door of McDonald's as she was settling the boys in when I saw a Japanese man walking toward me. Erm, well, OK, I saw a *lot* of Japanese men (and women) walking toward me but … I immediately recognized one man's face.

I was completely baffled; I was sure I knew this man, but I couldn't figure out who the heck he was. He wasn't one of my students from Fujisawa, but I didn't know anyone else in the country. We locked eyes as he approached, and we kept our eyes on each other as he kept walking. It was really bugging me that I didn't know why I recognized him. Just as he walked past me enough that we both would have had to turn our heads to maintain eye contact, his name jumped out of my mouth. "WATANABE-SAN!" I hollered. He immediately turned and came to talk to me.

Back in Canada, in the six months that I was waiting for my work visa to be processed, I had started to take basic Japanese lessons so that I knew at least a bit of the language before arriving in Japan. Our teacher was a lovely woman who brought us snacks and once took us on a field trip to a Japanese restaurant for lunch to introduce us to the food. She also brought in a guest speaker on one occasion to talk to us about Japanese culture—a fellow from Japan who had recently moved to Canada.

Here he was. Standing in front of me. Outside of a McDonald's. Somewhere in Ōsaka. Why?

We chatted for a few minutes. He was in Japan for a short trip, leading a student group on a study tour. And he happened to be walking past *that* McDonald's at *the* moment I was waiting for two little

Canadian boys to be strapped into their strollers. If my friends and I had been ten seconds later exiting McDonald's, this chance meeting would have never happened. Watanabe-san would have been among the sea of people without my even knowing he was in the country.

The second piece of bread in this bizarre coincidence sandwich happened two-and-a-half years later, a few weeks before my contract in Japan ended and I moved back to Canada. Maya, my new Canadian co-worker who had replaced one of my other co-workers, told me there was a new Canadian teacher in a school about half an hour away, and someone would be hosting a welcome party for them a few nights later. I was already in exit mode, not necessarily wanting to meet new people that I wouldn't see again, but I figured it would be fun and it was better than staying home doing nothing.

A few nights later, Maya and I hopped on the train to go to the party. The house where it was held was only a few minutes' walk from the train station, but it was pouring rain and cold that night—only a few degrees above freezing—because it was early February. The moment we walked into the warm house, my glasses fogged up and I couldn't see a thing. I had barely, blindly folded up my umbrella when I heard a loud male voice very close to me exclaim, "OH MY GOD! IT'S YOU!" Suddenly, I felt strong arms wrap themselves around me in a huge bear hug. I had no clue who was smothering me. I giggled and apologized, "I can't see a thing, so I don't know who you are!" The arms released me, and I took off my glasses, wiped them off, and put them back on. My jaw dropped when I saw who was in front of me.

The university I had graduated from four years prior had around 3,000 students total, so the same people were often in classes together. We also saw the same faces walking down the hallway; even if we never talked to certain people, we all knew each other's faces. There, standing in front of me at this house party in the suburbs of

Tōkyō, was a fellow named Damien, whom I had had several classes with. Until that night, however, we'd never had a conversation with one another. I knew his name from hearing professors calling on him in classes, but he was someone I passed in the hallway for four years and had only ever said hello to. There he was, beaming at me as if I were his long-lost best friend. I burst out laughing and we had our first conversation. (And, as it turned out, our last.)

I still remember the names of these two men. I still remember exactly what they looked like. And I haven't seen either of them since.

CHAPTER 2

LEARNING THE ROPES

Personal Touches

In the early 1990s, Fujisawa (a forty-five-minute train ride from central Tōkyō) had about 300,000 people. Technically, this was a "small" city in the Tōkyō suburbs. Indeed, the town was quiet and homey compared to the hustle and bustle of Tōkyō, but when looking out the windows on that forty-five-minute train ride, passengers would never see a break between towns and cities. The only indication of no longer being in Tōkyō was that the buildings got shorter and slightly more spaced apart. Everything was all one big city at first glance, but upon digging deeper, the differences started becoming clearer. One such difference was in the size of apartments.

My apartment in Fujisawa was big by Japanese standards, boasting two rooms. Penny, my Canadian co-worker, who lived in the same apartment building as I did, only had one, as did Brian, an American fellow I trained with in Tōkyō a few weeks after arriving.

About a year after Brian and I arrived, he moved from his apartment in one area of Tōkyō to another. His new location would be a better option since it was closer to his school.

As the only person he knew with an international driver's license, I was summoned to help him move. I drove the little rental van down the left side of busy, narrow streets in Tōkyō from his old apartment to his new one—which WAS newer and closer to his school, but ... smaller. Much smaller. As soon as he entered his new apartment, he burst out giggling at its size. Brian was about six feet tall. He immediately tested the size of his place—which was all of one room plus a small bathroom—by standing dead center, leaning out, and touching each of the four walls without moving his feet. Yep, I was living in luxury in comparison.

My kitchen was off to the side of the main, bigger room, the latter being a little smaller than an average Canadian living room. Inside the front door of my apartment was also a smaller room. If I were thinking of it in Canadian standards, that smaller room would be an average-sized walk-in closet, but I'm pretty sure it was meant to be a bedroom. My hotel room on those first few nights was similar in size to this "closet." I did sleep in the alleged bedroom for a while, but after I had been in Japan for a few months, I bought a small metal couch with cushions for my living room. It folded down into a bed, and I used it as both a couch and a bed rather than sleeping on my futon on the floor.

I initially loved sleeping on a futon, but after the first few months, I wanted to be off the ground. My main incentive for moving off the floor occurred one night while I was sleeping on my futon. I felt something in my hair and batted at my head only to realize a cockroach was crawling around in there, likely because he liked the smell of my strawberry shampoo. Still half asleep, I grabbed the vacuum cleaner, which happened to be right beside my head, turned it on, and sucked him out of my hair with the hose before rolling over and going back to sleep. Time to buy a bed.

After acquiring the couch, I used the smaller room as a closet and storage space. Over the three years that I stayed in Japan, I moved my little couch-bed from one wall to another any time I wanted to redecorate. Before I had the little couch, though, I bought myself some other furnishings.

My apartment was "fully" furnished when I moved in. My school provided the apartment. (I had to pay the rent but they had secured the lease.) It also supplied basic appliances and furnishings: refrigerator, toaster oven, one pot, one pan, two forks, two knives, two spoons, a couple of plates and cups, a *kotatsu*,[8] and a futon. Michelle had not cleaned the apartment before vacating. After cleaning it up and getting settled, I decided that I needed a few extras since the apartment was furnished with only the basics. I packed my camera, wallet, and an extra jacket into my backpack and went down to the beach to hang out before going shopping.

The beach was a thirty-minute train ride from my apartment, and another ten minutes' train ride east was the small city of Kamakura, home of the *Daibutsu* (Great Buddha statue) and other significant historical and cultural sites. "From 1185 to 1333, Kamakura was the *de*

---

[8] Kotatsu: a small, square table, roughly coffee-table height with a heater under the removable tabletop. Since Japan does not use central heating, a kotatsu is a cozy way to read, eat, or do anything at a table while staying warm. A blanket goes under the tabletop and above the heater, and the heater is plugged into the electrical outlet on the wall. The blanket then drapes down to the floor, keeping the heat trapped. Users can sit (on the floor) at the kotatsu with the blanket covering their legs, thereby keeping their lower body warm.

facto capital of Japan as the seat of the Kamakura shogunate. It also became the nation's most populous settlement from 1,200 to 1,300 during the Kamakura period."[9] After being in Japan for several months, I bought a bike and most weekends during my stay, I would ride it down to the beach and then along the shore on the path through Kamakura. The city and the shoreline are beautiful, and the biking or walking path along the coast was easy to ride on.

On this particular day, I spent some time walking the path along the beach, snapping pictures, and exploring. On the way back from the beach, I got off at the main train station (one stop before my home station). From there, I walked to Topos, a four-storey discount department store similar to Walmart, situated roughly halfway between downtown Fujisawa and my apartment.

On one floor of the store, I stumbled upon some comfy-looking red cushions, roughly eighteen inches square, that I thought would be perfect to use when sitting at my kotatsu. I grabbed two of them. On to the next floor. There, I hunted down a clock and placed it in my basket. Floor number three was where women's clothing was sold. I didn't desperately need any clothes, but I knew I would quickly blow through the several pairs of pantyhose I had brought with me. I didn't trust that Japanese pantyhose would fit me, so I grabbed only one pair to try them out.

A little bit of this, a little bit of that, some kitchen utensils, linens, and so on. I filled my basket, made my way down to the first floor, and found the cashier. As I plopped my cushions down on the counter and proceeded to empty my basket, the young woman working

---

[9] "Wikipedia: Kamakura." Wikimedia Foundation. Last edited September 1, 2021, 04:05. en.wikipedia.org/wiki/Kamakura

at the till looked at me quizzingly and her facial expression told me her internal voice was saying, "Eh-h-h-h-h-h-h-h....?"

I had done something wrong. I paused.

Hand gestures politely flying hither and yon and words quickly following led me to deduce that possibly I was to pay for the items on the floor where I had gotten them. Yep. That was the case. And so I had a puzzle to solve—trying to remember which floor each item had come from. After all, it's not like I could read the signs indicating what types of goods were sold on each floor. Sigh. I began escalator-hopping, carrying armloads of almost-purchases, which I then had to sort through on each floor to ensure that all items *were* ultimately paid for.

Up to the top floor, then down the escalator, stopping at each floor, sorting, and paying. Learning how to shop at a Japanese department store would come in handy for the future since Topos quickly became my go-to place for household necessities. Besides this, though, my reward for enduring this ordeal was a humongous clear plastic bag that I could put all of my purchases into since most of them didn't fit into my backpack.

I finally had everything paid for and thrown into the monstrous plastic bag. Time to go home. My apartment was about a twelve-minute walk away.

The bag was too big and too heavy to carry in one hand. My first thought was to drag it, but I knew dragging it on the cement would quickly tear the bag, rendering it useless. My only option was to sling the bag over one shoulder, Santa Claus style. This seemed appropriate, considering the main contents of the clear bag were the two VERY RED cushions, which were suddenly a lot heavier than I realized when I had picked them out. I hoisted the bag over my shoulder and headed out for home.

It started raining!

Well, with the bag being quite heavy and the rain pelting down, the bag kept slipping out of my hands, so I stopped every minute or so to switch hands and shoulders and to attempt to get a better grip on the bag. Red traffic lights were a welcome break even though stopping for them meant getting more soaked.

Home seemed awfully far away that day. By the time I arrived, I was sopping wet, exhausted, and past the point of caring about all of the strange looks I received all the way home. The important thing was that my beautiful new red cushions were dry.

How Many Gaijin[10] Does It Take to Screw in a Light Bulb?

Everyday tasks are a challenge when living in a foreign country, especially a country that has a starkly different culture from your own.

Not even three weeks after my arrival in Japan, two light bulbs in my apartment burnt out. When one considers the life span of a light bulb, the odds that two of my six bulbs would burn out in my first three weeks in a new country were theoretically not terribly high. But burn out they did, and so a dilemma ensued: how to change these light bulbs.

One of the light bulbs was built right into the ceiling of my hallway, much like a pot light, and the hole that the bulb was in was barely big enough for me to get my hand into. But not out of. Why is it you can always get your hand INTO a small space but not out of it?

---

[10] Gaijin: foreigner. Gaijin is made of two words: gai, which means outside, and jin, which means person. Some people consider gaijin to be offensive or a bit crass; the more polite term is gaikokujin.

After much twisting and turning and puzzling and squirming, I was able to free my hand from the hole. Coming out of the hole with my hand was part of the socket, which I assumed was meant to happen. The removal of the mysterious piece of socket allowed me to put my hand back in and easily unscrew the light bulb.

Now, this wasn't your average Canadian 60-watt light bulb; it was just as mysterious-looking as the piece of socket that had come out when removing my hand from the hole. I took the newly-removed light bulb downstairs to the convenience store on the first floor of my building and played the "I can't see the difference; can you see the difference?" process-of-elimination game to buy what I was sure was the right type of bulb. I went back up to my apartment, screwed the light bulb in, put the socket piece back in place, and flipped the switch. Light. Hooray! One down.

Replacing the second light bulb wasn't quite as ... straightforward. It was in the living room ceiling and near the built-in wall cabinets that lined my hallway. My apartment was on the top floor of the building and the ceilings were high—about twelve feet high. The main room in my apartment was sunken, so the hallway and kitchen floors were higher and therefore closer to the ceiling than that of the main room. The cabinets in the hallway stretched from the floor to about four feet below the ceiling. It was ironic that my light bulbs were so far out of reach. I was in a country where so much was done on the floor—sleeping on a futon, drinking tea and eating at a kotatsu, reading and relaxing in *zaisu.*[11] The only things in my apartment that had legs were me, my kotatsu (slightly less than knee-height), and the

---

[11] Zaisu: a Japanese chair with a back and seat but no legs, so the seat sits on the floor. Often used with a kotatsu. I didn't have zaisu and therefore bought the red cushions, but zaisu are comfortable and provide back support.

cockroaches—and I knew the Archies[12] weren't going to be any help changing the light bulb.

I moved my kotatsu to the end of the hallway near the dead light bulb. Hopping from floor to kotatsu to kitchen counter to the top of the cabinets in the hallway would have been great introductory training for future military service had I been so inclined to ever be athletic. I made it to the top of the cabinets unscathed. Whew! I sandwiched myself on top of the cabinets, reached forth, and unscrewed the light bulb. Victory! Until I realized I had neglected to bring the new light bulb with me. Sigh. Down I went. I grabbed the new bulb and jumped, stretched, and lifted myself back up to the top. Screw, screw, screw. I clamoured back down to the floor. Flick. Ah, success. And I hadn't fallen and broken my neck.

The Great *Gomi*[13] Dilemma

Taking the garbage out for weekly pickup used to be so much simpler in Canada in the '90s. But here is one of many areas of life in which Japan was years ahead of Canada (at least my part of Canada). In the late '80s and early '90s, as a university student, I separated my garbage and kept boxes of cans and cardboard in the storage room to be taken to the recycling center. Japan, however, already had recycling

[12] Archy: reference to poet Don Marquis' characters Archy—a cockroach—and Mehitabel—a cat—who "wrote" satirical, free-verse poetry. Archy was a philosophical cockroach who had been a poet in a previous life. penguinrandomhouse.com/books/227131/archy-and-mehitabel-by-don-marquis/

[13] Gomi: garbage

pickup as part of the weekly garbage services two decades before Calgary implemented it.

Again, I instinctively tried to apply my Canadian way of thinking to garbage-pickup day in Japan. Taking out the garbage should not be a big deal. After all, it just entails putting the garbage into a bag and putting it on the curb on pickup day, right?

Nope.

I was aware that there were certain days for picking up certain types of gomi. My manager and co-workers at school had given me the quick and dirty intro to the basics of separating my garbage. They informed me that:

- burnable was to be separated from non-burnable
- paper was to be separated from non-paper
- recyclable was to be separated from non-recyclable
- decomposable was to be separated from that which lives forever
- Canadian garbage was to be separated from Japanese garbage
- garbage generated in the daytime was to be separated from garbage created after dark
- blue and yellow garbage shall never be mixed for fear of it turning green
- cockroaches one had vacuumed from one's hair in the middle of the night were compostable but the bag inside the vacuum cleaner which contained said cockroach was not

The criteria seemed endless and thoroughly confusing. I was sure that on every day of the week, some sort of garbage was being picked up but the burning question was, WHICH DAY WAS BURNABLE GOMI DAY? For the life of me, I couldn't figure out and keep track of the schedule.

The only hope I had of being enlightened failed me. Penny, the other Canadian teacher at my school, told me that on Monday and Thursday nights, she simply took her garbage out, and the next morning it mysteriously disappeared. She didn't concern herself with separating her garbage into the endless types. She'd been in Japan for a year and a half by this point and hadn't been hauled away to gomi jail, but I wanted to be more conscientious than she was.

However, I had stockpiled ten to twelve big black bags of garbage from the initial cleanup of my apartment, and I decided it was time to start disposing of them. When cleaning up, I hadn't yet been oriented to the fact that garbage had to be separated and put out on certain days, so I had paid no attention to what was in each bag when I was cleaning. After I was finished, I knew that each bag contained a mishmash of "whatever had to be disposed of" and I was past the point of willingly opening all twelve bags to sort garbage. Each bag contained burnable and non-burnable items. Some contained paper AND non-paper (gasp!). Others contained Canadian, non-decomposing, non-burnable, no longer needed but not totally useless, partially broken but capable of being fixed, green, red, and *maybe even blue* garbage. And somewhere amidst the gomi pile was the one bad seed—a wee aerosol can that someday soon would quite possibly cause some poor, unsuspecting, lovely Japanese garbage man putting garbage bags into the incinerator on burnable day to exclaim, "*NANDARŌ*[14]... THAT WASN'T BURNABLE!"

Chōgo Chōgo Chōgo

After taking the train to and from work for three weeks, I had gained confidence in my ability to get myself back and forth, and I began to take for granted the fact that if there was a train waiting at the station, surely it must be there waiting to take me home! Now, I'm not naive enough to get on any old train. (Although years later, on my first trip to Germany, I almost ended up taking my mother from Frankfurt to Switzerland instead of Leipzig. We were on the right platform but far too early for our train). Of course, there were specific platforms for trains going north and different platforms for the trains going south, and I had quickly discerned which platform was the former (north being the direction of my station).

My workweek was Tuesday to Saturday, from noon until 9 p.m. One Thursday evening, Ken, my American co-worker and I, left work together and headed to the train station deeply engaged in conversation. I lived a few blocks from the first stop, which was a five-minute train ride away from the main station. Ken's place was several stops farther down the same train line in the next city, around thirty minutes away. We got on the same train, gabbing away, and found a seat. We continued blathering until a few minutes after the train had left the station, I saw Honmachi (my station) whizzing past us. NANDARŌ!! I asked Ken what was happening, and he innocently informed me, "You're on the express train," while giving me a look as if to say, *You*

[14] Nandarou: What???!! (What the hell?)

mean you didn't know? Um, why would I get on an express train? He knew where I lived.

Panic set in, but Ken reminded me that there is a solution to every problem—and the solution to this one was simple.

"Just get off at Chōgo, the first express stop. Go across to the other platform, and catch the next train back," he advised me. He also gave me some advice for the future: "You can tell the difference between the trains because express trains have red lights on them."

Fantastic.

The next night, I left work solo at the same time Ken and I had left the previous night. A train was about to leave the platform—a train that had red lights on it.

Cool. Since this train had red lights on it, I was obviously fine to take the next one, which didn't have said red lights.

Except ... I got on the next train, and moments before it left, I heard the announcement: "Bla bla bla bla bla bla bla bla bla bla bla bla **CHŌGO** bla bla bla bla bla bla bla bla bla bla bla bla." (I was still fairly illiterate at this point, so I couldn't understand either the writing on the trains or the announcements.) The mention of Chōgo caught my attention so I got off, looked at the train again, saw numerous other red lights, and looked at the schedule on the board on the platform. This train was listed in red on the schedule whereas others were in blue, so I concluded I had made the right decision by getting off this train before it left the station. Yep, I had been looking at the wrong lights. I was learning!

But I still had a way to go before I became a genius. The next night, a Saturday, I left work early. (Shortly after 9 p.m. was early; it usually took me thirty to sixty minutes to wrap up after the last lesson of the night). Just as I got to the station, whistles announced that a train was getting ready to leave, so I sprinted across the platform, briefcase flying, and flopped onto a seat on the train just as the doors were closing. No time to be observant.

Fifteen minutes later: hello, Chōgo … again! Whoops!

Leaving on the Midnight Train from Pukesville

Catching the last train at night, especially on a weekday, likely meant that the passengers were there for the same reason: they had been out and about socializing. Going to an izakaya or *karaoke* studio[15] after work with colleagues and clients, usually for several hours, is common in Japan. And there's always a fair bit of alcohol involved. The blood-alcohol level for driving in Japan is low—0.03 per cent—and the penalties for drunk driving are harsh. In light of the amount of drinking that takes place in these social and business outings, it's probably good that so many people rely on trains for transportation rather than driving.

Drinking culture is clearly defined in Japan, whether it be for alcoholic or non-alcoholic drinks. People fill each other's drinks (tea, beer, etc.) rather than filling their own, and no one takes a sip until everyone's glass is filled. To fill your own glass or to take a sip before everyone is ready to do so is considered rude and flies in the face of Japan's deeply rooted sense of collectivism and respect for others. Once everyone has a beverage in front of them, members of the group

---

[15] Karaoke: A popular form of entertainment in Japan, karaoke is different there than in Canada. Friends, colleagues, business people, and clients will gather and go to a karaoke studio, where they can rent a private room by the hour and sing together. Karaoke studios offer room service for drinks and food.

simultaneously raise their glasses in the air, call out *kanpai*[16], and start to drink. Completely emptying your glass or cup signals that you are ready for more. Your companions will keep pouring as long as there is space in your glass to pour into, so if you want to quit drinking for the night, you need to leave your glass fairly full. Otherwise, it will be filled for you. I was forewarned that many a foreigner mistakenly empties their glass of beer only to find it immediately filled and then the vicious circle beings because we westerners are of the mind that we don't leave our plates or glasses full. As a foreigner in Japan, trying to empty your glass before leaving a party is a battle you will always lose.

Ken was hanging out at my apartment one night, and as usual, we got to talking and lost track of time. As 12:30 a.m. approached, we realized it would be wise for him to head to the train station to catch the train home. I walked Ken to the station, and his train was arriving as we got there. He slipped his monthly pass into the machine to open the entrance gate, passed through the gate, retrieved his pass, crossed the overpass above the train tracks, and descended the stairs to the platform on the other side. After all that, he missed his train. Fortunately, there was still one more train to come, so he waited on the platform while I waited outside the entrance, where I could see but not hear him.

Ken was the only person waiting for the first several minutes, and I continued to wait with him to make sure there was, indeed, one more train. A middle-aged Japanese man dressed in a business suit arrived on the platform and waited for the train, as well. As I was waiting, I could hear this man loudly and repeatedly clearing his throat and coughing from across the rails while he paced back and forth acting strangely.

---

[16] Kanpai: cheers!

Gross and weird, I thought to myself.

I noticed Ken slowly moving farther and farther away from this man toward the opposite end of the platform. The next day I got the story as to why.

Turns out this other man was more than a little drunk, and the throat clearing wasn't exactly that. Ken told me that what I couldn't see was this man was shoving not one but both fists into his mouth, forcing himself to gag and puke. What I also couldn't see was that the man was making piles of puke, one by one, moving down the platform, which was why Ken kept inching his way down the platform away from the man.

The next day, however, the puke piles were all gone. Apparently, someone working for transit had a nasty job description.

Miso[17] Rice and Other Assorted Delicacies

One of the biggest adjustments when living in a different culture is adapting to the food. The typical food of one culture is, of course, strange and sometimes off-putting to those from other cultures. But as someone who was brought up on a cattle ranch and ate copious amounts of beef tongue, *prairie oysters*,[18] and chicken feet in my first eighteen years, I have always been pretty open to trying new foods. I'm a big believer in trying something before passing judgement on it. I was a tad relieved to see a McDonald's and KFC across the street from my

[17] Miso: a Japanese seasoning made from fermented soybeans and sometimes rice, seaweed, and/or barley. Miso serves as the base for miso soup, which accompanies many Japanese meals.

[18] Prairie oysters (also known as Rocky Mountain oysters): fried calf testicles. A delicacy in ranching communities.

school when I first arrived, and those places did come in handy in times of comfort-food emergencies. But I wasn't completely opposed to trying raw fish and raw horsemeat.

The majority of Japanese food is delicious, fresh, and healthy.

I had tried some at a Japanese restaurant in Alberta a couple of times before moving to Japan, but I stuck with what I had heard of before: teriyaki, noodles, etc.

In my first week after arriving, I was taken out almost every night after work by students and co-workers who wanted to welcome me. My students, in particular, wanted to order their favourite dishes so that I could try the foods they were so proud of. I continued to force myself to eat the sushi so as to not offend anyone. Magically, and for reasons that escape me to this day, after about the third time eating the sushi my students had ordered for me, something instantly switched to the "on" position within my brain. Sushi became one of my favourite Japanese foods. To this day, it's one of my favourites of all kinds of food and is something I eat often.

I have, however, never had sushi as fresh as I did at an izakaya about two years into my stay when I was out with a group of students who ordered for me. Shortly after they ordered, one of the servers approached the fish tank inches away from my right arm, retrieved some fish out of the tank (splashing my arm in the process), and then returned to our table moments later with a plate of fish that was ... still twitching. My students insisted I eat it quickly. I popped it into my mouth with my chopsticks, mentally patting myself on the back for having come so far—from being squirmy about putting raw fish in my mouth to appreciating and enjoying the fresh taste of a fish that was still moving in my mouth.

On my first full day in Japan, I had been treated to a lunch of *tonkatsu*,[19] and it immediately became one of my favourite Japanese foods. Shortly thereafter, I was excited to discover a takeout restaurant only two blocks from my school that sold tonkatsu *bentō*[20] boxes. Ordering from this place on my lunch breaks and taking the bentō back to my school to eat became a weekly habit.

The first time I bought the bentō, I took it back to school to discover the pork was placed on top of the shredded cabbage with a wee package of the beloved tonkatsu sauce inside one of the two wee boxes. The other wee box—a bit wee-er than the other—contained some plain, short-grained, steamed white rice topped with some black stuff that was kind of slimy but tasty. (I later discovered these shreds of slipperiness were black seaweed.) The rice was also accompanied by a small package containing a dark-mustard-coloured paste. Since I still couldn't read much Japanese in any of its written systems, I used the powers of deductive reasoning. The box containing the pork contained the pork sauce, so naturally, this package in the box with the rice must contain a sauce that is to be put on the rice. Perfectly logical, right? So I opened the package, squeezed the sauce onto my rice, and tried it, discovering that it was a delicious add-on to the rice. I thought it was strange that this sauce was so thick, but I reminded myself that I was in a different culture. Perhaps putting a thick, pasty substance on their rice was normal to Japanese people even though I found it odd.

I continued my weekly ritual of buying the same bentō—pork, cabbage, rice topped with seaweed, and accompanying sauces—and

---

[19] Tonkatsu: deep-fried pork cutlet topped with a tangy, brown sauce. Usually served with a side of shredded cabbage, a bowl of plain steamed white rice, and a bowl of miso soup.

[20] bentō: a boxed takeout lunch

dutifully continued putting the sauces on the appropriate accompanying items.

After several weeks of performing and confidently perfecting this ritual, I was pressed for time one day and rushed out to buy my bentō. When I returned to the school, I quickly started downing it in the short time I had remaining before a group lesson. Two of my students were early. When they arrived, I was finished eating everything except the rice, so I quickly grabbed the little package of "sauce," opened it, and started squeezing it onto my rice.

Shrieks and eardrum-breaking "E-H-H-H-H-H-H-H-H-H?"s followed, courtesy of my students. Something was wrong.

"What? What?" I asked them.

"You're putting that on your rice?" they asked me incredulously.

"Yes, it's delicious. What? Am I not supposed to put it on my rice? What's wrong?"

They informed me that the package contained miso paste. Squeeze it into a bowl, add hot water, and stir. Voila: miso soup.

One of those students, Masayo, was a giggly, fun junior high school-aged student at the time who has since become a great friend of mine. She informed me in January 2021 when I was fact-checking some of the information for this book with her that the convenience stores now have miso rice balls for sale … and she likes them. Huh. It took Canada twenty years to catch on to iced coffee, which was popular in Japan well before I arrived. But now that we have adopted iced coffee, it seems Japan has embraced my miso rice idea. (See, Masayo, I was on to something! I was just a little ahead of my time.)

日本

A few years after I moved back to Canada, I inadvertently got my revenge on Masayo for her shrieking in horror at my putting miso on my rice. She came to Calgary to visit, and one of my best friends and I took her to a Japanese restaurant downtown. By this time, I was well aware that to Japanese people, putting anything other than salt and perhaps sesame seeds or a few strands of seaweed on plain steamed white rice (especially soy sauce, which we love to do in North America) is utter blasphemy. Japanese people consider white rice to be pure and holy; to them, putting soy sauce on white rice would be like a westerner putting ketchup on a really nice piece of Pacific salmon or Atlantic lobster. While out for dinner with Masayo, as soon as our food arrived, my friend promptly grabbed the soy sauce to put on his plain white rice and was met with the same shrieks and "E-h-h-h-h-h-h-h-h-h???!!" that were directed at me when I put the miso paste on my rice in Japan years earlier. My friend was a little confused at Masayo's reaction, and of course, I burst out laughing and roared heartily.

Masayo has the greatest sense of humour, and we still laugh loudly together when reminiscing about these incidents.

CHAPTER 3

THE GOLDEN WEEK

Golden Week, the week of April 29 to May 5, is one of the biggest holiday periods in Japan. It includes four national holidays,[21] and everyone seems to be on the move during that week, travelling to other parts of the country. Besides national holidays, I only had ten vacation days per year of my contract in the first two years (minus any sick days I took). I was eager to take advantage of the stretches of national holidays to travel within and outside of Japan. The problem with Golden Week is that everyone else is travelling, too, so trains, flights, and accommodation are booked solid well in advance.

Exploring Mountain Regions

Ken and I decided to explore Japan a bit during this first Golden Week for both of us. (He had arrived in Japan and started working at

---

[21] For more information, visit "Golden Week in Japan" at tripsavvy.com/golden-week-in-japan-1458351.

my school only six weeks before I did.) Both of us were young and overconfident, thinking we could easily get ourselves from Point A to Point B. With our accommodation and train tickets booked well in advance, we set off for Nagano *prefecture*,[22] a mountainous region north of our prefecture (Kanagawa). Several years later in 1998, the winter Olympics would be held in Nagano.

To catch our train to our destination town, Chino, we had to wage war on Golden Week crowds at Shinjuku station in Tōkyō, the busiest train station in Japan any day of the year (and, allegedly, the busiest train station in the world).

We met up at Yamato's main station early enough to ensure that we wouldn't miss our *shinkansen*.[23] Yamato was the city where Ken lived, half an hour north of Fujisawa's main train station. We arrived in Shinjuku an hour early, around 8:30 a.m.—which, in my opinion, was about two hours too early to be up and mobile on any day. (The noon start of my job agreed with me, as I am not a morning person.)

With an hour to spare, we decided to first find the platform where we were to later catch our shinkansen. Mission accomplished: the platform was a short walk through the station and around a corner from where we had disembarked the train that brought us there. No problem.

Because we had both left home early in the morning, what little breakfast each of us had had was long in the past, and our stomachs were talking to us. We went on the hunt for something to eat. Breakfast ended up coming from a small coffee shop a few steps away from the

[22] Prefecture: a governmental region or district in Japan—similar to a county, state, or province.

[23] Shinkansen: Japan's famed bullet trains, which travel up to 320 kilometres (or 199 miles) per hour.

platform we needed, so we each grabbed a couple of doughnuts, a coffee, and some snacks for later.

We quickly ate our doughnuts, and Ken suggested we trek to *Kinokuniya*, a huge foreign bookstore, to browse. I had no idea where the bookstore was, but Ken was sure it wasn't far from the station. He looked out the windows at the mass of Tōkyō "skyscrapers."[24]

"I'm not exactly sure where it is, but it's not far from here," he tried to assure me. "Maybe about a ten-minute walk."

I looked at my watch. 8:55. Thirty-five minutes until our train departed. I subtracted twenty minutes *minimum* for walking to and from the bookstore, combined that with flashbacks of my first week in Japan trying to find my hotel, and decided I wasn't terribly desperate for books.

"We'd better not chance it," I decided for the two of us.

So we loitered around the coffee shop until about fifteen minutes before our train departure. Thinking we would be really on the ball, we decided to head to the platform a little early.

We approached the ticket gate and presented our tickets to the attendant. Problem. He wouldn't let us pass through the gate. Ken and I looked at each other, both of us hoping the other would know what the problem was. Nope. The line-up of people behind us was rapidly getting long and people were getting pushy, so we exited the line and used our best body language to ask another gate attendant what the problem was. He was quite fluent in body language himself and somehow managed to convey to us that we had only one of the two

---

[24] Buildings in Japan, even in Tōkyō, are not nearly as high as they are in other countries because of the frequent earthquakes, but Tōkyō is a dense and bustling city.

tickets required to get us through the gate. Neither of us had known that we needed to not only book the reservation but the actual seat, as well.

Our next problem was finding the wicket where we could buy the other halves of our tickets. We had ten minutes till departure, and being the worrier that I am, I was also concerned about having enough cash. Our initial tickets had cost us about ¥30,000 (around C$350 at the time). Who knew how much this extra ticket would cost? I only had another ¥30,000 on me, neither of us had a credit card, and we needed money for food for the next three days.

After wandering around for a few minutes, we found the ticket booth. Five minutes and ¥2,500 (about C$30) later per person, we passed through the gate and found our train.

Chino is a small town about two-and-a-half hours northwest of Tōkyō by train. We settled into our seats and got comfortable, armed with paperbacks, a deck of playing cards, my Scruples card game (a terribly important item I had included in all the luggage I had brought from Canada), and our snacks. The male half of this travelling duo wanted to get right to the meat of the matter, ordering me to pull out my Scruples game even before I could find a place to set my backpack for the trip.

"If you were the president of a large corporation which had recently …." We didn't play Scruples according to the rules, but we used the questions in the game to get to know each other better and pass the time. We picked each other's brains for about an hour, sometimes surprising each other with our answers, and then took a break. On the windowsill went the cards, out of the backpack came more munchies, and into my book went my nose. After about ten minutes, I dozed off.

When I awoke, we were about two hours into the train ride with presumably half an hour left to go. Ken wanted to pick up the Scruples cards again, and so the discussions resumed. The train made a stop, and I heard the conductor announce that Chino was the next stop. According to my calculations, we would be stopping at Chino in about twenty-five minutes.

Ten minutes later, we were engaged in a heavy debate as the train started slowing down. We paid no attention until I thought that looking at the signs out the window might be a good idea. Sure enough, I saw a sign labelled "Chino" just as the train stopped.

"This is it! This is our stop!" I hollered at Ken, grabbing everything in sight. The train only stopped for a minute or two at each station, so we had to be quick or we would end up who knows how much farther down the line.

"What? What?" Ken hadn't seen the Chino sign and therefore had no idea what was happening. Like me, he thought we had another fifteen minutes or so until arriving. Fortunately, he allowed me to pull him out of his seat and push him off the train. As the train pulled away, there we stood on the platform, my backpack slung over my shoulder, both hands full of juice boxes, snacks, cards, books, and garbage. Ken looked dumbfounded, asking, "Where are we? Is this our stop?" Apparently, in his mind, I'm the type of person to suddenly throw a fit and toss someone off a train just for laughs.

"Are you sure this is our stop?" he kept asking me. "I didn't hear them say 'Chino.' This better be our stop, because if it isn't, we have no way of getting to our stop." He was starting to make me doubt myself. We walked about ten steps down the platform past a sign that said "Chino."

At that, he believed me.

The Fume Room

The language school where Ken and I worked owned small resort homes called Wellness Clubs[25] at various spots throughout Japan, which were available at a fairly low rate for staff members to use on vacations. Ken and I had booked spots at our company's Wellness Club in Chino. When we got off the train, we looked for a taxi to take us to the Club since that was the only way to get there. We arrived after a thirty-minute, C$60 taxi ride.

The house was comfortable with space for twelve to fourteen people, depending on how many people shared each of the multiple bedrooms. The place was empty when we arrived, but we found a sign that other humans had arrived before we did: fresh food in the refrigerator. We gave ourselves a quick tour and placed our bags in the biggest and nicest of the empty bedrooms, claiming it as ours. Ken went into the bathroom to have a shower while I stashed our food into the remaining space in the fridge. I then set out to explore the house a bit more.

It was a beautiful and cozy building. I loved each of the *tatami*[26] bedrooms. The only room bigger than ours was a loft overlooking the living room, and it had already been claimed. There was another room labelled "The Workroom," which contained a number of long tables and a moveable whiteboard. Ken, myself, and the other humans we met after they came back from their walk decided that this room bore too much resemblance to a classroom and was therefore to be avoided at all costs. This was the Wellness Club, and we were there to get well, which required us to have no reminders of work. Whiteboards were

---

[25] The official name of these resorts

[26] Tatami: traditional woven grass mats used for flooring in Japan

outlawed. We closed the door to that room and none of us set foot in it during our time there.

The room Ken and I chose had what seemed like a big water stain on the tatami in one of the corners. No big deal; we didn't need to use the corners of the room. After surveying the rest of the house while Ken was in the shower, I was satisfied we had chosen the best room available and went back to our room to shuffle through my luggage.

Ken's shower ended up being a long bath. While he was idling away and I was getting us settled in, I discovered that the water stain on the tatami was not a water stain. As I sat on the floor rifling through my backpack, I became increasingly aware of a turpentine-like smell. Upon closer inspection of the stain, I realized that it was, in fact, a gas stain. At some point, gas had leaked out of the heater, which was mounted on the wall near the ceiling in that corner of the room, completely saturating one of the tatami mats and partially soaking two others. The fumes were suddenly quite strong, and I realized that if I slept in that room, I would get sick with horrendous headaches.

Knocking on the bathroom door, I informed Ken that I was going to move my bags to a different room and explained the reason.

"Move mine for me, too," I was instructed. So I dragged our belongings up the stairs into a smaller but also cozy room with clean tatami.

A few hours later, our housemates returned, and we collectively decided that it would be in everyone's best interest if we removed the gas-soaked tatami mats and cut off the gas supply to the heater in that room. It had never occurred to me how heavy a tatami mat might be, much less one that was saturated. The three stained mats were beyond rescue and would have to be replaced, so we didn't worry about lugging them out onto the balcony to be further drenched by the rain that was pouring down by this time. A great start to our vacation: terrible weather and gas fumes in the house. Ken and I asked the other three vacationers if they smoked. Fortunately, none of us did, thereby greatly reducing the risk of the house blowing to smithereens should someone light a match.

We were left with two rooms being out of bounds: The Workroom and The Fume Room.

Ken and I ended up only sleeping one night in our little tatami room. Shortly after we had arrived, six young Japanese people drove up in a car and claimed the other three smaller rooms. A married American couple arrived late the first night to find that all of the rooms had been claimed except for the gassy room. (We had all made reservations through a central booking office prior to Golden Week, so the house was fully booked. However, taking the stinky gas room out of the mix meant the house was one room short for all the bookings. We had no idea how to resolve the issue other than sort it out amongst ourselves.) The last arrivals insisted on everyone keeping their rooms and offered to sleep in The Fume Room with the windows open to diffuse the gas fumes that lingered. The next day, however, yet another married American couple arrived. Five minutes after they arrived, the husband looked at Ken and told him, "There are no empty rooms. My wife and I have nowhere to sleep." We could tell immediately these were the kind of people who would complain about a grain of rice being too small. To ward off any unnecessary drama over the next few days, Ken and I promptly went into our room, dragged our futons out, and slept in the living room the final two nights we were there.

Trust

Ken and I had one common goal for this vacation: to climb Mount Tateshina, elevation 2,530 meters. We were mountain goats, so to speak—between his being from Montana and my being from Alberta, we had both spent a lot of time hiking in the Rockies. Our hiking boots were among the first items we had both packed for this trip. Unfortunately, it rained off and mostly on for the first two days. Since we had to leave on the fourth day, we decided that our last full day would be the best day to conquer the mountain. Even if it were still raining, we agreed we would attempt the hike on our last full day since we had no other options to do the hike.

By this time, we were both sleeping in the living room, Ken on the couch and I on the floor beside the patio doors. Someone had left the curtains open before we went to sleep, so bright and early on Friday morning, the sun jabbed us in the eyes. We woke up to discover a thick blanket of snow on the ground outside. I had hiked in snow before, but this stuff was the slippery, dangerous sort, not the sticky, crunchy kind, and I didn't have crampons.

"Forget it," I said to Ken as I threw the blanket over my head and immediately became anti-social.

Ken, however, was determined to climb the mountain and proclaimed that he was prepared to go by himself. For someone determined to go alone, though, he was sure trying to convince me to join him.

"You'll regret not trying. You'll probably never get to this part of Japan again. This is our last full day here. This is the only chance you'll get to climb this mountain. I'm gonna go. If you don't want to, I'll just go by myself. But you'll regret it if you don't go."

From under my blanket, I considered the time, distance, temperature, and clothing involved.

Well, I mused from beneath my fortress, *if the snow has melted a couple of hours from now, I'll go. If we leave at 10 a.m., we should still be able to do it, but if we leave any later, we'll be coming back in the dark. I'll wait as long as ten and then decide.*

I remained under my blankie for a while, then rose to get showered and dressed.

By the time I was presentable, the futons were put away, and we had had breakfast, it was nearing 10 a.m. and the snow was gone, although the ground was still wet. But it was a sunny day. We decided to give Mount Tateshina a go, so we geared up and left.

Off we went with no map and no compass—armed only with sandwiches, oranges, juice, a couple of bananas, my formerly solid but rapidly depleting sense of direction, and Ken's complete lack of the latter. Neither of us took any money along; we couldn't imagine needing any. We knew in which general direction the trail for Mount Tateshina was, so we headed due … "that way."

Anytime I have gone hiking, I have driven to or been dropped off at the trailhead and taken off on foot from there. Not owning a car in Japan forced me to improvise in several ways in a myriad of situations, and this hike was one such scenario. To get to Tateshina, Ken and I had to scale a smaller ridge, cross a highway, and then find the trailhead.

Two hours after starting out, we were crossing said highway. Looking for the trailhead. Arguing over whether to go right or left. We found a small ... *something* that looked like a parking lot, and a big brown sign in *kanji*.[27] The trailhead was nowhere to be seen.

"Let's just bust through the underbrush and head straight up the mountain, then."

(One guess as to whose idea that was. A two-word hint: NOT MINE!)

However, there seemed to be no other viable option, and so a-trailblazing we went. All the while, I was looking for a trail, and at one point, I thought I could see one to our far right.

"Wait! Stop! Look over there," I hollered. "See where there's a kind of break in the trees? I bet that's a trail."

"Well, why don't you go and see?" Ken was about forty feet to the left of me.

Go and see I did. It was a trail.

HA!

"It's a trail!" I hollered back at him.

"Well, does it go up?" he queried.

"It's gotta be the trail to Tateshina. There's no other trail around," I insisted.

"Well, I'm not going over there unless I know it's the RIGHT trail. Why don't you follow it for a couple of minutes and see where it goes?"

Follow it I did.

---

[27] Kanji: the Chinese characters that are also used in written Japanese

"It goes around that way," I pointed to the right, hollering back at him again.

"Well, that's going in the opposite direction. It can't be the right trail."

"Well, where would it go if it doesn't go up Tateshina? There's no other trail around." I wasn't giving up.

"It goes back into those hills," was Ken's (un)educated answer.

OK, I had done enough hiking in the Rockies by this point in life to know that trails dip and dive. They go down before they go up; they go left before they go right; they zig and they zag; they surprise you before eventually taking you where you are intending to go.

"It's gotta be the trail," I insisted. I had no proof, though. I just had my gut feeling. "It probably turns right a bit here and then veers off left and then up the mountain." My arguments were starting to sound pathetic even to me.

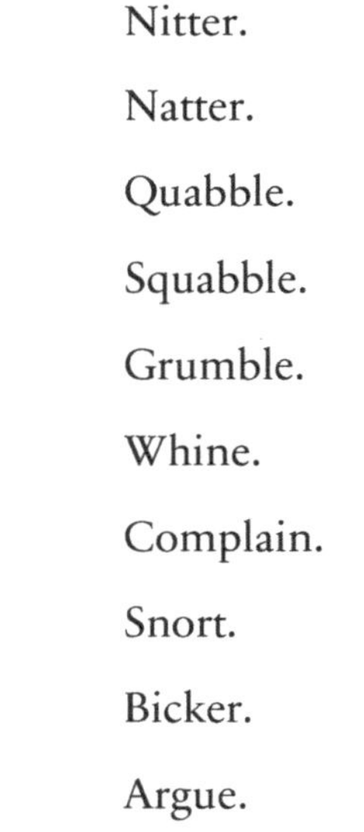

Nitter.

Natter.

Quabble.

Squabble.

Grumble.

Whine.

Complain.

Snort.

Bicker.

Argue.

He wouldn't trust me.

"Well, I'm going to follow the trail myself then," I announced. "It's a lot easier than trying to get through that crap you're busting through." I could barely see Ken's hat above the grass.

He pondered the situation.

Hem.

Haw.

He shifted from left foot to right foot. Then back again.

"I'll come," he finally relented. "I'll trust you on this, but if this trail leads nowhere, you owe me a beer."

"And if it goes up Tateshina, you owe me three beers," I accepted his bet.

"If you find a trail that leads to the top of this mountain, I will gladly buy you three beers."

Deal.

I waited a few minutes until Ken caught up with me, and then we started off together. We walked about eight feet, and then the trail veered sharply to the left. There, in front of us, in all its glory, was the face of Tateshina and a distinguishable trail heading all the way up the mountain from where we stood. I started salivating, looking forward to my free beer.

Tateshina was an enjoyable hike. It reminded me of the Rockies except for the lack of wildlife; we didn't see so much as a bird! It was challenging, as any hike to the top of a mountain is, and I didn't make it all the way to the summit. I stopped about forty-five minutes short of reaching the top. I was starting to get tired, and I wanted to save my energy for the hike back since we did not have access to a car to take us from the trailhead back to our accommodation. We were already about four hours in and we still had to turn around and go back.

Ken went on to the top himself while I flower-picked my way a little further up the trail and through the snowpack until I decided I wanted to plant my behind on a rock. After sitting there for about half an hour, I was getting too cold to just sit so I started to slowly descend the mountain, checking behind me now and then to see if Ken was on his way back.

At one point, I caught a brief glimpse of him up the mountain until he disappeared again behind some trees, but I continued, assured that I wouldn't be making the trek back to the house alone. Before long, I heard someone running in the snow behind me. I stopped to wait for him.

The first evidence I saw of any type of live creature was a human arm attached to a plaid umbrella. I was momentarily confused. I was sure there was no one else on the trail, and neither of us had brought an umbrella. (Why would *anyone* take an umbrella hiking with them?) Someone obviously had, but we hadn't seen another person for hours. Within moments, I saw that at the other end of the umbrella was my friend, and I immediately asked him how on earth he came to possess it.

"I found it on the summit. Someone must have forgotten it there," he replied triumphantly. He was grinning like a five-year-old who had just won first place in a finger-painting contest.

日本

At this point, I need to enlighten you as to the reputation Ken had established with our co-workers and friends. Since arriving in Japan less than four months prior, he had lost no fewer than five umbrellas. He'd developed a habit of leaving them at izakaya, at karaoke studios, and on trains. He had quickly become known among our co-workers and his students for being absent-minded in general, and he was already the regular recipient of pity and compassion for always being umbrellaless. The irony of him finding an umbrella ON THE TOP OF A MOUNTAIN, and one in perfectly good condition, was not lost on me.

日本

After I laughed and rolled my eyes at Ken and we both caught our breath for a minute, we continued on our merry way down the mountain. Since going down is always faster than going up, we made good time. The fact that the sunset was quickly approaching was added incentive to get our butts off the mountain and at least get close to the Wellness Club before it got too dark.

Down Tateshina we went, across the highway, and up to the top of the smaller ridge we had scaled at the beginning of our journey. We were moving fast by this point and had only stopped briefly to allow cars to pass on the highway between the two mountains. When we got to the second ridge on the side of the highway nearest to the Wellness Club, we saw a small shelter and stopped there briefly to down the last of our oranges. We had also hiked that ridge two days earlier, so we were on familiar turf at this point, and I wasn't worried about getting stuck outside in the dark anymore. We relaxed a bit and then set off again.

Being utterly exhausted after pushing ourselves up and down two mountains, and bushwhacking a good portion of that, we stopped again after about twenty minutes for a final rest. As we surveyed the landscape and watched the sun start to go down, Ken suddenly had a realization.

"Where's my umbrella?"

I looked at his hands. The umbrella was no longer extending from his arm.

We combed the ground and peered down the trail behind us. Nothing in sight.

I squinted and looked back to the shelter, twenty minutes into our past. Flashback. Just before peeling our oranges, Ken had hung the umbrella by its handle on the balcony of the shelter. It was surely still there.

I don't know if it was the exhaustion, the relief of having (almost) conquered the mountain after waking up to snow and not being able to find the trail, the lunacy of the whole umbrella situation, or a combination of all three. Whatever the reason, I suddenly found the situation to be completely hysterical. I spent the next ten minutes rolling around on the ground in fits of laughter. Four months and now six umbrellas—including one he was in possession of for mere minutes on these mountains before he lost it.

Night was coming, so after I caught my breath and stood up, we took off along the ridge. Before long, the resort area was below us and buildings were in sight.

"The Wellness Club is white with a red roof, so it should be easy to find." Words of wisdom from Ken.

I looked down.

Directly below us was one house. It wasn't white, and it didn't have a red roof. We couldn't see any building that matched the description of our temporary home.

Great.

Dusk had come.

"Why don't we just keep going on this trail instead of going down here?" Ken suggested. "The trail will get us closer to the Wellness Club than if we go down now, and it will be easier to find the Club from up here if we can see the colour of the roof."

While this seemed logical, my gut instinct was screaming at me otherwise. However, I decided to give Ken the benefit of the doubt and follow his reasoning. I had, after all, been hard on him all day.

Eventually, the trail veered off in the wrong direction, so we backtracked a little. Ken stopped.

"That looks like the Wellness Club over there." He pointed toward one of the red roofs. Terrific. First, there were no red roofs; now, there was nothing but. "Let's drop off here. We should be able to cut straight across to the house."

So we dropped off the ridge. Twenty minutes later, we were in someone's backyard with both of their dogs barking at us in Japanese.[28]

Neither of us had any idea where we were, and by this time, it was pitch dark. We decided to rely on our lacklustre sense of direction to find home. After *another* twenty minutes, we were in the middle of nowhere again with nothing in sight but a lonely police booth. Fortunately, this lonely police booth contained a lonely police officer. Unfortunately, neither Ken nor I had a bilingual dictionary with us. In our best, horrible Japanese, we explained to the officer that we were lost and were trying to find the Wellness Club.

Twenty minutes later (I have no idea why, but at this point, everything had to happen in twenty-minute intervals), the police officer

---

[28] In English, dogs say woof woof or bow wow, but in Japanese, dogs say wan wan.

phoned the service center [29] of the resort area to ask where our company's house was. No one at the service center knew where our house was, but someone *did* know that one of our housemates was currently in the center. And it just so happened to be the only housemate with a car.

The police officer took us to the service center, and the housemate took us back home. Thus, we arrived safely home from a gruelling day of hiking and arguing, two hours after sunset. Without Ken's new umbrella.

How I Spent My Golden Week Vacation

Ken and I returned home, me to Fujisawa and him to Yamato, after a restful and fun vacation. The weather had been inclement and there hadn't seemed to be much to do in the Chino area other than go hiking. No matter. We both loved hiking, and the mental break in the Japanese countryside was rejuvenating.

On May 6, we were back to work. Golden Week was over, and every person in Japan was back from their travels. My students were eager to share their Golden Week stories and to hear mine. Many of them had only had three days off whereas I had had the whole week.

One of my students told me of a particularly exciting festival she had witnessed during her Golden Week travels. Anthropology is a huge interest of mine, so I was eager to hear about this festival. And when she told me about it, I was jealous that I had missed the chance to see something so spectacular.

---

[29] A sort of information and help center

In this festival, a group of men climb to the top of a mountain and ride back down on a huge log. Ropes are attached to the log for the men to hold on to, yet every time this festival is held, some of the men are killed because of the massive log blasting at high speed down the mountainside. My student informed me that this festival takes place only every six years and is, understandably, quite spectacular and exciting to see. With my plan to be in Japan for between two to five years, I wouldn't have the opportunity to see this festival the next time it was held.

"Where is this festival held?" I asked her.

Her reply: "Chino."

CHAPTER 4

SUMMER BRINGS MORE FAILURES

Browbeaten by a Japanese Toilet

Japan has always been years ahead of Canada regarding its nifty technological gadgets. Current innovations such as the wide-eyed robots we see on the news these days are fascinating indications of the potential of science and invention. Many of these innovations start out as fun toys but then eventually become integrated into mainstream society. When I was living and teaching in Japan in the early '90s, I was awestruck by some of Japan's cutting-edge technologies that I had to learn so I could maneuver through everyday life.

Two of my favourite advances that Japan had over Canada when I lived there were touch-screen ATMs and vending machines that sold both hot and cold coffee. The first time I approached a touch-screen ATM in Japan, I remember being both confused and intrigued.

It took some poking and pondering, but once I got up to speed on how to use these machines, I was enthralled. To be depositing and withdrawing cash from a machine with just the light touch of my index finger on the smooth screen seemed so futuristic. When I came back to Canada in 1995 and was forced to use the ATM keypads reminiscent of Touch-Tone telephones, I felt as though I had time-travelled by decades to a previous generation. For the almost twenty years it took until touch-screen technology came to Canadian banks, I missed the sleek design and the smooth feel of the touch screens. For three years, they had transported me into my own private sci-fi banking scene.

During my first few months in Japan, I was amazed to see the array of items available in vending machines: batteries, pornography, comic books, porn, cups of instant ramen, porn, beer, porn, lots of porn. Of course, the usual chocolate bars, chips, and soft drinks were available, but I was fascinated that canned coffee was also available in some vending machines. First and foremost, whoever had the idea of putting prepared coffee into a can and selling it was a genius as far as I was concerned. Easily accessible and portable coffee! But then, to sell it both hot *and* cold! I had never heard of drinking chilled coffee, and I had also never seen a vending machine selling hot drinks. My head was spinning from the choices.

I quickly discovered that cold coffee, especially in the summer, was as satisfying and delicious as hot coffee could be. It took me a lot longer, though, and much trial and error, to know whether the coffee I was selecting from the vending machine was hot or cold. Sometimes I got what I wanted and sometimes I didn't. I finally figured out after several random selections that I need only look at the colour of the kanji lettering under the coffee: red = hot, blue = cold. Again, genius! Even though I couldn't yet read the characters, I took comfort in realizing that someone was obviously was looking out for me by implementing this colour coding. My only jobs were to do the decoding and make my selection.

Overall, the Japanese language is not as difficult as it appears at first glance. The writing system is actually quite straightforward and fun. The greatest challenge lies in learning the kanji. Kanji are numerous and can seem complicated, but after learning the first batch of basic characters (numbers, days of the week, basic nouns, etc.), finding patterns in the more complicated characters and puzzling them together become easier. Kanji is quite logical and fascinating, especially for visual learners.

Three of us on our staff of twelve were not Japanese: me, Ken, and Michelle, who was from Toronto and hereafter referred to as Michelle No. 2 (not to be confused with Michelle-from-Philadelphia, hereafter referred to as Michelle No. 1, whom I replaced!). This Michelle had arrived five months after I did and replaced Penny, who left that summer. One evening, Tomoko, one of our Japanese co-workers, had invited the three of us to her home for an evening of visiting and enjoying some snacks and beverages. She lived with her parents, as is the custom in Japan for unmarried women and firstborn sons, although this is changing. All three were typical gracious, polite Japanese hosts.

Naturally, at one point, I had to use the toilet.

Bathrooms in Japanese homes are usually just that: a room with a bathtub. Toilet rooms are often separate little cubbies with only the toilet and a sink. My hosts' toilet room was just off the living room, where we were all seated, and I went into the toilet room to do my business.

I had a rudimentary reading ability in my first few months in Japan, so trial and error combined with deductive reasoning became my go-to approaches for getting things done, such as learning to choose my vending-machine coffee. I certainly had no idea how to approach the space-age toilet that I was confronted with in this room. Most toilets in Japan have two buttons on the top of the tank: a larger button for "big flush" and a smaller one for "little flush." This toilet did not have those buttons. However, it had a plethora of other unique functions and options as indicated by all of the push buttons on the armrest—yes, it had an armrest! The seat was heated (lovely!), but other than assuming that the red and blue buttons were temperature control for the seat, I had no idea what all of those buttons were for.

Naturally, the push buttons were labelled in kanji, which at that point I was able to read at roughly a kindergarten level. Unfortunately for me, the days of the week were not among the array of characters on this toilet. I was left feeling illiterate and helpless, not to mention disappointed that I couldn't test out this porcelain spaceship without potentially instigating an international incident.

What does this button do? I wondered as I sat there, admiring and inspecting the options available to me. I didn't dare touch anything because I really had *no* clue what any of the buttons would do if I pushed them. I didn't want to inadvertently launch myself into space with my pants around my ankles. How embarrassing would *that* be?!

After doing up my pants, I turned around and leaned over the bowl of the toilet to get a closer look at these buttons. Since I couldn't understand any of them, I had no idea which button said "flush." By the powers of deductive reasoning, I concluded that since "flush" was the most common function on any toilet, the largest of these buttons would certainly be "flush."

I triumphantly pushed the largest button and heard *bzzzzzhhhhhttt* quietly coming from inside the toilet bowl.

Suddenly, I was assaulted with a spray of water blasting directly into my face. My glasses were immediately covered and I started spitting back the water that was pelting into my mouth. In my panic to avoid the spray, I instinctively stood up, throwing my arms up to try and block the water from hitting my face. This only resulted in the sleeves and front of my shirt getting doused. I had no idea what was going on. Why was this toilet, in The Land of Ultimate and Eternal Politeness, attacking me when all I had done was appreciate it for keeping my bum warm while I was sitting on it?

As quickly as it started, the spray stopped, and I heard another *bzzzzzhhhhhttt*. I took off my glasses in time to see the little bidet spout retreating to under the back of the toilet seat where it had been hidden from sight until I had awakened it.

I was dripping from the top of my head to my waist. Utterly soaked. While trying to get my head around what had just happened, I cleaned myself off as best I could with the towel. In doing so, I noticed out of the corner of my eye the good old-fashioned silver flush handle on the side of the toilet where it is on all Canadian toilets. I defeatedly pushed it to finish my job.

Now what? Even though I had wiped myself off as much as I could, my hair and shirt were a dead giveaway that I had been the victim of a brief and mysterious downpour in the toilet room. I couldn't very well stay in the room long enough to let my hair and shirt dry; I had already been in there long enough that I was sure everyone was wondering what I was doing. Drawing in a heavy sigh, I opened the door and re-entered the living room, embracing my blunder and facing Tomoko's parents and my co-workers.

"Well, we don't have toilets like THAT in Canada ...!!!"

Foojed

A wise man climbs Mount Fuji once, but only a fool climbs it twice.

I had heard this Japanese saying before I even left Canada. Being an avid hiker and knowing that Mount Fuji was climb-able, I had put it on my list of fifty things to do before I die, which Colleen had encouraged me to create on the flight between Vancouver and Tōkyō.

The climbing season for Mount Fuji is short, though. Snow comes early and stays late on this technically still-active volcano (although it hasn't erupted in more than 300 years). We've all seen the stunning pictures of this majestic mountain with its trademark snowcap. I have always been under the impression that hikers are only allowed to climb Mount Fuji in July and August, but it seems that doing so in other months is possible, just not recommended. Facilities are not open during winter months, though, and of course, climbing in the winter when the mountain is covered in ice and snow is much more treacherous than in the summer. There were therefore only a few weekends in July and August in which I could plan to climb it. The limited "open" climbing season also meant that almost everyone in Japan who wanted to climb it was also gunning for trail space on those same weekends.

My opportunity came the first summer that I lived in Japan. Brian, my American friend who lived in Tōkyō, was interested in climbing it, too, and neither of us had anything else planned for the last climb-able weekend in August 1992. It was time to be wise.

The typical approach is to start hiking around 9 or 10 p.m., which slots the five- to seven-hour climb perfectly so that hikers can reach the top in time to see the sunrise. We decided to buck the system, however, and climb during the day. Through a series of phone calls in the week prior, we arranged to meet at Shinjuku station at 8 a.m. that

Sunday, take the train to the foot of Mount Fuji, hike during the day, and be back home at night. Both of us had Sundays and Mondays as our days off, so our plan would give us Monday to recoup and be perky for work on Tuesday.

On Sunday morning, I got up and took the forty-five-minute train ride to Shinjuku station. When I got off the train, I found the meeting spot that Brian and I had agreed on and waited.

And waited.

And waited.

I looked at my watch.

8:25.

8:30.

8:35.

He was nowhere to be seen. I wandered a bit looking for him, but I didn't want to stray too far since I was at the agreed-upon meeting spot and I didn't want to miss him when he did eventually show up. I waited for about another hour until I finally gave up.

I took the train back home, extremely annoyed that my only shot at climbing Fuji that year had been blown because Brian had, for some reason, not shown up. There was no way I was going to embark on an escapade like that on my own.

When I got home late that morning, I immediately picked up the phone and called him, ready to blast him for standing me up.

"Where were you?" I accused him.

"I was there! Where were you?" he countered.

"What? I was there by 8 a.m. and waited till almost ten before I came home!" I retorted.

He insisted he was there. Impossible. I mean, Shinjuku is a busy station, but he was a six-foot-tall Caucasian guy; he stood out from the crowd, even in busy and multicultural Tōkyō. There was no way he was at the same place I was without me seeing him.

He described where he was standing, and I did the same. Erm … turns out he was on the second level and I was on the first. I guess we had failed to clarify which level of the station we would meet at; we had only decided on which exit.

"So what now?" I asked. "This is the last weekend to climb Mount Fuji for this year. We really can't go tomorrow and be back in any shape to work on Tuesday."

We quickly agreed that we did want to give this a shot. Rather than waiting another year, we decided to nap a bit and try again to meet up later in the day and climb at night, as was the popular course of action.

"OK, I will have a nap and then see you later on the second level," I clarified, then hung up the phone.

I retired to my futon.

I tossed. I turned. I tossed some more. I couldn't sleep. Even though I had set my alarm, I was probably afraid of not waking up in time. That, along with the excitement of actually climbing this iconic mountain, kept me up all afternoon, and I just wasn't tired enough to fall asleep. By the time I had to leave for Tōkyō for the second time that day, I had been up since 5 a.m. It was going to be a long night.

Within minutes of getting off the train in Shinjuku, I found Brian, and we headed to the ticket machines to buy our tickets to

Kawaguchiko, where we would disembark and begin our climb. The train ride from Shinjuku took roughly a couple of hours. We had timed our arrival having back-planned: if sunrise was around 5 a.m., and the climb would take five to seven hours, we aimed to be on the trail and trekking by 9 p.m. We wanted to give ourselves a bit of extra time for breaks since we knew it would be a gruelling climb.

Right on schedule, we started at the trailhead along with a bazillion other people. This was not going to be a relaxing hike. Nope, we were part of a mob that was all there for the same purpose: to enjoy the sunrise from the top of the highest mountain in "the land of the rising sun." I decided to accept the fact that we would be in high traffic the whole way. After all, this wasn't a hike for the sake of enjoying the scenery and some serene, quiet nature. This was an ACCOMPLISHMENT. We had a job to do.

There isn't much to say about climbing Fuji, especially at night. It isn't scenic, even in the daytime. It's rocky, barren, dusty, steep, boring, and ugly. Because it's a volcano, there's sharp volcanic rock everywhere. The beauty of Mount Fuji is seeing it from a distance, but it's a bear when your feet are on it. It's a slog. The climb is tedious, crowded, and tough. Climbing it is definitely not something to do for enjoyment. It is all about seeing the sunrise from the summit.

Up. Up. Up. Switchback after switchback. The grind was relentless on the legs and the butt and the lungs. Several sections had poles dug into the ground a few feet apart, with chains strung along the top so that climbers could use the chains to pull themselves along. I found the chains to be great for balance and a bit of support in the steeper sections.

Each station marked the end of a section and the beginning of another, much like how the climb from Mount Everest Base Camp to the summit is divided into camps and then steps. On Mount Fuji, huts dotted the way at several stations. The huts were only open during the short climbing season in the summer, but when open, they offered tea, snacks, and space on the floor where climbers could sleep along the way. It is also well known that the higher the station, the higher the price for these items.

We slogged along past station after station, slowly getting more tired but realizing that with each step we were getting closer to the summit. Then it started to rain. And the fog rolled in. Even though it was the dead of night, and therefore pitch dark, we could tell that the fog was getting worse. Our flashlights served us well, and the throngs of other people also carrying flashlights helped us find our footing. But as we climbed higher, the fog got thicker. We got more tired and progressed more slowly. The combination of having been awake for more than twenty hours at this point plus the strenuous climb and the depleting oxygen levels as we got higher were starting to rapidly knock me out. I had to stop more and more often for breaks, and I could tell Brian was getting impatient with me. Finally, when we reached the last station before the summit, I told Brian to go ahead without me. I didn't want him to miss the sunrise because of me, and I was rapidly losing interest in making the summit anyway. He went on ahead.

What I hadn't confessed to Brian was that I wasn't confident I could get to the top and, more importantly, I was starting to completely not care if I did. The fog continued to thicken, and I had come to terms with the fact that there was going to be no sunrise to be seen from the top anyway because of the inclement weather. Still, I was this close; when I did the rough calculations, I figured I was just under 500 meters from the top. I trudged on, thinking this would be my only shot at checking "climbed Mount Fuji" off of my list. The lack of sleep and the thinning of oxygen, however, were starting to become too much to overcome. I got to the point where I was taking three to five steps and then having to stop for ten minutes to rest. It was a strange feeling; I had never felt the energy zapped from me in that way before. After five steps ... rest for ten minutes ... repeat a handful of times, I admitted defeat and decided I had no desire to die on that mountain. Getting to the top, even though I was probably only about 200 hundred meters away, was not going to happen. It wasn't worth pushing myself over the edge to summit a mountain in the middle of a huge crowd of people and a massive cloud of fog. I started back down.

I knew Brian would be well behind me because he was determined to see the sunrise. That was still about an hour away, so I stopped at the first hut on my descent and shelled out some cash to grab a spot on the floor and catch an hour of sleep. After a good power nap about that long, I got up and resumed the trek back down the mountain. The sleep had served me well. The fog hadn't lifted in the least, and it was raining pretty steadily at this point, but with my renewed energy, I merrily trucked down the mountain.

When I got to the trailhead, I found a spot out of the way so as to not be trampled by the throngs of people coming back down, and I waited for Brian. He appeared about an hour after I had gotten to the bottom, excited that he had made it to the top in time for the "sunrise," which, in the fog, was merely a gradual and slight brightening of the sky. I was excited I was still alive. We both slept soundly on the train ride back to Tōkyō.

In the years since then, I have always told people that I climbed Mount Fuji but quickly clarified that I didn't quite make it to the top. Did I conquer the mountain or did it conquer me? Probably the latter. But in the end, I have no regrets that I made it so close to the top without getting all the way there, especially since there was no sunrise to be seen that day anyway. As far as I'm concerned, under the circumstances and considering my struggle, I was being wise.

The Great Fujisawa Steak-a-Thon

My twenty-third birthday came along several months into my first year living in Japan. By then, I had hit a few bumps in the typical culture-shock roller coaster, but I had settled into my job and was loving both the work and my students. As a private language school, our employer had no problem with us socializing with our students after hours and, in fact, encouraged us to do so. We weren't expected to, but it was also a great chance for us Canadian and American teachers to learn more about our adopted home while getting to know our students better. The vast majority of my students were adults, and most were older than I was. I built friendships with many of them. They were wonderful, generous people who were excited to teach their culture to me, Ken, and Michelle No. 2. I enjoyed and appreciated their enthusiasm for taking me to festivals, tourist attractions, and cultural events, and they were eager and proud to take us to them. Going out together for lunches or after-work drinks at izakaya or karaoke was also a lot of fun.

Two of the students in my most advanced class wanted to celebrate my birthday with me. Toru was not only my student; he was also my neighbour. He lived only a few blocks from my apartment. Knowing that I came from a cattle-ranching background and therefore loved beef, he had a suggestion for my birthday.

There was a great little Mexican restaurant two blocks from my apartment. The food, while not terribly authentic, was excellent, and after I had been there only a couple of times, the staff treated my friends and I like family. My first time there, I'd noticed the perimeter of the room had vertical, yellow strips of rectangular paper hanging along the wall just below the ceiling, each one with different Japanese writing on it. Some of them had the words "Give up" written on the bottom in English along with the Japanese writing.

While chatting with Toru after class one day, I asked him what those strips of paper were for. He explained that the restaurant had a promotional deal. They had a two-kilogram steak meal, including a small corn salad, and whoever could eat it all in thirty minutes (or less!) would get it for free. Anyone who tried and failed had to pay for it; the price was the equivalent of about C$60.

I joked that it would be funny to try to conquer the steak. The joke became a reality.

Completing this challenge for my birthday was Toru's idea, and he promised that if I tried it, so would he. Akiko, a perky high school girl in the same class as Toru, jumped into the conversation and said she wanted to try, as well.

And so I had plans for my first birthday in Japan.

Akiko, Toru, and I would be attempting to down the massive steak. Michelles No. 1 and 2 and Ken would be spectating and cheering us on. I didn't train for this event. I figured being a rancher's daughter from Alberta, the home of great beef, was training enough. I did, however, starve myself throughout most of the day so that I would be good and hungry by evening.

I walked down the street to the restaurant, both dreading and looking forward to what the evening entailed. I mean, I loved beef; how hard could it be to eat two kilos of it? (I didn't have a good grasp of how much that actually was). But I also remembered that almost every one of those yellow strips had "Give up" written on the bottom.

Akiko and Toru were pumped up, and the other three were delighted to witness this historical event. We ordered our food, much to the delight of the staff, who had had no prior knowledge of our intentions. And we waited.

Shortly thereafter, the server brought forth six sizzling and monstrous plates of beef, each with one kilo of steak, and three small bowls of corn salad. The bowls were about the size of a small pickle dish and held probably about half a cup of fresh corn salad. On every other visit to the restaurant, I had looked forward to the corn salad. Looking at it beside the spread of beef, though, it seemed unnecessary and evil.

We quickly scrambled to clear everything off the table that didn't need to be on it—basically, everything except the massive spread of beef and the tiny bowls of corn salad. Then we grabbed our forks and knives in our fists, stared each other down, and got ready for the signal to start eating. The other three in our group cleared well enough away from the table to give us room but remained close enough to take pictures and perform their cheerleading duties. The entire table was covered in beef, and the server gave us our instructions:

"You must eat all of the beef and the corn salad within thirty minutes or less."

Now that I had a visual of just how much meat we were talking about, I knew this would be impossible, but we were past the point of no return. Akiko, however, was still claiming she could do it.

"And GO!"

We started sawing away at the beef. I had no idea what kind of strategy to employ, so in the interest of saving time, I decided the best approach was to streamline my time by quickly cutting and then putting a piece of beef in my mouth, then cutting some more while chewing so I could keep my molar assembly line going.

Fifteen minutes in, I was starting to feel full. Really full. Toru was sweating. Akiko was happily plugging along as if it were any other meal. I was in awe of how she was just taking it all in stride, and I was quite perplexed at how much she seemed to be enjoying the process when Toru and I were already struggling. Michelle Squared and Ken were dutifully cheering and laughing and taking pictures.

Fifteen minutes down, fifteen to go.

None of us was anywhere near being half done with our meat at this, the halfway point of the time limit. But I was not about to give up. Nope. The other two were still eating, and my competitive nature kicked in.

"Don't forget about the corn salad!" Michelle No. 1 taunted us.

Oh, yeah. The blasted corn salad.

I took a bite of the corn salad. It seemed to be a waste of time and stomach space, but it was, after all, part of the deal. I begrudgingly downed most of the salad.

A small drink of water washed everything down, and I resumed cutting the steak. My pace was slowing considerably, as was Toru's. Akiko showed no signs of stopping or even slowing down.

Ten minutes left.

I had to take a break, even for just a few seconds. My jaw was getting sore from constant, rapid gnawing, and I was past the point of being slightly uncomfortably full. But I would not give up. Even though in my mind I had already admitted defeat, I was going to keep pushing through to the thirty-minute mark, as were Toru and Akiko.

Five minutes left.

Looking down at my plates, I realized I was going to be doing well if I made it through half of my steak. Another couple of bites of corn salad and the bowl was empty.

A few more bites of steak, a slight pause, and a few more bites.

And the countdown began.

"Five! Four! Three! Two! One! And stop!" (In honour of the birthday girl, the staff counted down in English.)

I thankfully put my fork and knife down and let out a huge sigh.

Toru and Akiko looked equally relieved.

"Oh my God. I'm so full," I moaned while the spectators laughed.

Toru was sweating even more by now, and Akiko was still smiling and giggling even though she admitted she was also "very, very *ippai*."[30]

Suddenly, I was desperate to go home. I did not feel well at all and I just *really* wanted to lay down. That damn corn salad had surely put me over the edge.

We paid our penalties and left. The short walk home felt endless. When we got back to my apartment building, which was on the way to the train station, I quickly thanked everyone and headed up the three flights of stairs to my door. I couldn't wait to lay down.

I never did throw up; I just lay on my futon for more than an hour staring at the ceiling. I've overeaten at other points in life, but not to this extent. It was an awful feeling—like someone had stuffed a rock inside my belly. I couldn't move for a while. I knew that after I eventually fell asleep, I would feel better the next day. In the meantime, I just wanted to rip all of the meat out of my stomach, but I also didn't want to throw up. I remained planted on the futon until I felt well enough to get up and get ready for bed, and then I went to sleep.

---

[30] Ippai: extremely full. Onaka ga ippai: my stomach (onaka) is full.

For the next two-and-a-half years, every time we ate at that restaurant, I looked up with pride at the one strip of yellow paper on the wall that stood out from the rest because the name on it was in *katakana*[31] rather than kanji: "ローナ スチューバ[32] Give up."

---

[31] Katakana: one of three written Japanese alphabets or scripts

[32] ロ-ナ (Ro-o-na) スチュ-バ (Su-chu-u-bah); my name as pronounced and spelled in Japanese

CHAPTER 5

EXPATS ON THE LOOSE

Fall of my first year rolled around. By this point, I had met and solidified friendships with several other Canadians and Americans teaching in schools within a forty-five-minute train ride from where I worked and lived. Most of these other twenty-somethings were teaching for the same language company that I was, and whenever a new teacher arrived, the existing network reached out to welcome them. Social groups shifted as teachers left and new arrivals appeared.

I had met a lot of foreign English teachers in my first few months, but my core group of friends settled into the two I worked with (Ken and Michelle No. 2) as well as six others, some of whom also worked together. We formed a little gang of silliness and spent the next couple of years hanging out together.

All of us worked Tuesdays to Saturdays from noon until 9 p.m. except Ken; he worked Monday to Friday. Our work schedule created one problem: On a Saturday night, once we got out of work and took the train anywhere to meet friends, it was well past 10 p.m., or even getting close to eleven. This gave us roughly an hour to spend together before having to catch the last train home. As a result, we ended up crashing at each other's apartments many Saturday nights so that we could play pool, sing karaoke, drive go-karts, or just go out for food and drinks until well past midnight. This beat rushing a short get-together and heading back home on the last train.

We were all recent university grads living abroad for the first time. While we had our differences, we were also pretty down-to-earth and our personalities clicked together well. We had all arrived within several months of one another, so everyone was experiencing the same stages of culture shock roughly around the same time. A fun, supportive, and active little group, we enjoyed Japan and wanted to take advantage of the opportunities the expat life offered.

All I Want for Christmas Is a Burger

As my first Christmas in Japan loomed, none of my friends planned to go home, and we started to talk about how to spend the holidays. A handful of us Canadian and American teachers, along with Tomoko, decided to head to Australia for the winter break.

Flights and hotel rooms were booked, visas were in our passports, and tentative plans were beginning to take shape for what to do while we were down under. We were flying directly to Cairns from Tōkyō. We figured we would have no trouble keeping ourselves entertained for eight days, what with the Great Barrier Reef to explore, so we planned to stay in Cairns rather than go to any other parts of the country.

Ken's main goal was to bungee jump. This was 1992, when bungee jumping was all the rage. Australia and New Zealand were the "cool" places to do a jump since those countries are where the obsession originated. No, thanks. You couldn't pay me enough to do something that reckless. I figured I would find enough hiking and other activities to do; he could do the wild stuff.

About six weeks before our trip, I got horribly sick with a sinus cold that I just could not shake. I would have three or four bad days, feel better for a day or two, but then get knocked right off my feet again. The weeks dragged on and I was not recovering. I went to two doctors and tried every cold medication I could get my hands on. Nothing worked. And I was having to sleep sitting up because every time I lay down, I couldn't breathe. It got so bad that I considered cancelling my trip to Australia. If I were sick the whole time, what a waste of money it would be to just lay in the hotel room, unable to do anything.

In the end, I decided to go. I was well enough to fly, for one thing. I also figured being in a warmer climate and an English-speaking country would relieve the pressure on me to constantly try to think in Japanese. This would give me the mental break I needed after ten months and at least make me feel a little better psychologically. And I wouldn't be alone and miserable for ten days. I would be with friends while being miserable and perhaps make them miserable, too!

And so I stuck with the plan. Since we were going to be in Australia over Christmas, the six of us going had decided to do a little Secret Santa gift exchange with a low spending limit, and we drew names a couple of weeks before leaving. I drew Tomoko's name. Since she had lived in the US for several years and loved American snack food, I decided to give her one of the many packages of Oreo cookies that friends and family had been sending me from Canada. (Everyone knew I liked Oreos and I had grumbled that they were hard to find in my city, so everyone sent me Oreos, which resulted in me eating so many Oreos that I subsequently began to dislike Oreos. Haven't touched them in years.) I wrapped up a package of Oreo cookies in Christmas wrap along with a small package of beautiful Japanese paper that I knew Tomoko would use since she did Japanese calligraphy. I packed her gift in my suitcase along with my clothes and toiletries.

The eight-hour flight from Tōkyō to Cairns was not pleasant. I was so sick with the sinus cold that I just tried to sleep and endure the flight as best I could. One advantage of flying to Cairns from Tōkyō was that the two cities are in the same time zone, so at least there was no need to adjust to a time change.

We landed in the early hours of the morning. After a restless bit of sleep on the plane and feeling like my head was about to explode, I was not in a good mood when we went through Australian customs. I figured since they were a commonwealth country and I was Canadian, they would be fairly friendly, but nope. They were direct, picky, and thorough. I was pulled aside and asked if I had brought any food into the country. I said no. When they opened my suitcase and saw the box wrapped in Christmas paper, I was instructed to unwrap it.

The agent saw the box of Oreos. "You said you had no food with you," he accused me gruffly.

I had completely forgotten about the damn cookies. Apologetically, I explained that I was part of a group of English teachers in Japan, the cookies were my Christmas gift for one of my travel companions, and I had forgotten about them. Perhaps my Canadian honesty came through, or perhaps he felt sorry for me and how sick I was. Whatever the reason, he softened after that, putting the cookies back into my suitcase and waving me on.

About ten seconds after clearing customs, the sinus headache that had been pounding at me for hours since leaving Tōkyō finally got the best of me. I ran to the corner of the room and barfed on the floor.

I immediately felt better; the pressure in my head eased up and my sinuses cleared. And oddly, I felt perfectly fine from that moment on for the rest of the trip.

A couple of us went to church in Cairns on the morning of the twenty-fifth. The minister was wearing a red-and-white Hawaiian shirt and Bermuda shorts, and it was nice to be somewhere warm and English-speaking after struggling through the language in Japan for the previous ten months. When I phoned home on Christmas Day to talk to my family, everyone on my mom's side of the family was at my parents' house. All fourteen of them. Everyone except me. It was the first time we all weren't together, and I was the culprit who had broken the chain.

My extended family was just sitting down to the turkey dinner when I called, and my mom passed the phone around so I could have a quick hello with everyone. That phone call left me with mixed feelings. Of course, I missed my family, and they were having The Great Turkey Dinner with everything that comes with the bird. (I'm one of these freaky creatures who loves Brussels sprouts and Jell-O salads AND fruitcake!)

Meanwhile, my friends and I were eating tomato sandwiches from the convenience store because nothing else was open in Cairns on Christmas Day. I was trying to convince myself that I had one-upped my family because it was -30 degrees Celsius at home and +30 in Cairns. And yes, we were spending the afternoon at the beach—but we couldn't go in the water because it was jellyfish season, and there were signs everywhere warning of their deadly sting. To add to the strangeness, while we were walking along the beach, a woman came along with her dog, who promptly peed on one of my friends' legs.

It wasn't the worst Christmas, but it was a bit lonely and odd.

日本

Several weeks before heading to Australia, I had done my duty and put together a fairly good-sized box of Christmas gifts to send to my family back in Canada. My mom received the box in time to distribute the gifts to my grandparents, my dad, and my sister. One of my expat friends had told me about a three-storey shop in Harajuku (a district of Tōkyō) called the Oriental Bazaar, which sold lacquerware, clothing, Japanese dolls, fans of all sizes, and tchotchkes of all types. The bazaar was the go-to place for high-quality Japanese souvenirs, so I did all of my Christmas shopping there, including buying a vase for my mom. When I saw the vase section, I thought, *Oh, what a great idea! These are beautiful, and Mom can use this for years to come.*

Well, I wasn't wrong there; she's using it forever. As it turns out, the "vase" I bought her was actually an urn, which we buried her in when she died fifteen years later. It wasn't until she received her gift that I got my answer to the question, "Why do these vases all come with lids?" Mom was the one who educated me as to what the "vase" truly was and therefore why it had a lid, but she loved it. She never did use it as a vase. The (empty) urn was displayed in her china cabinet for years until she ... ahem ... needed to use it. In those years, on occasion visitors would tentatively and respectfully ask her whose ashes were in it. Being as my family has a warped sense of humour, the "vase" was a source of a lot of jokes between me and my mom until she got her terminal cancer diagnosis. She solemnly informed me she most certainly wanted us to put her ashes into it. Still, when we buried the urn containing her ashes, I couldn't help but smile that the "vase" that she had loved for years was finally being put to use the way it was intended.

日本

By the time evening rolled around on the twenty-fifth, the local Japanese restaurant had opened for dinner service, so instead of being relegated to gas station convenience store sandwiches for the second time that day, we ate Japanese food. We were a little grumbly about that. Even though we all loved Japanese food, after many months (and for some, a little more than a year), we were starving, literally and figuratively, for a chance to be surrounded by more familiarity: English-speaking people, western food, and familiar customs. We did, however, enjoy the meal and focused on finding non-Asian restaurants for the rest of the trip so we could get our fill of homestyle food before heading back to Japan.

Teetering on the Edge

Ken had changed his plan. Bungee jumping was still something he wanted to do, but more than that, he wanted to get his scuba certification through PADI (the Professional Association of Diving Instructors). What better place, after all, to do scuba certification than the Great Barrier Reef? He registered himself for the program, which ended up taking him away from us all day every day except one, so he had to forego bungee jumping. On the only day that he was free, we all went whitewater rafting down the Tully River.

I was envious of him on all fronts. When I was a kid, I was enthralled with TV shows showing footage of scuba diving. I have always thought it would be so mesmerizing to be under the water—swimming with unique and colourful creatures, checking out corals, and looking for sunken treasure. Even now, the idea of scuba diving really appeals to me, but I am not convinced I would actually enjoy it because of my fear of water and my inability to swim well. Maybe someday I will muster up the courage to try, but in Australia, I tried snorkelling for the first time, and that was as far as I could push myself to confront my fear of deep water.

I was also—and still am—afraid of heights, so while bungee jumping was not on my list, I felt bad that Ken wasn't able to do it. My jealousy of his scuba outings on the reef and the desire to be more adventurous convinced me that I needed to consider this bungee jumping idea. I mean, *someone* in our group had to do it! No one else was interested, so I talked myself into "taking one for the team" and representing Ken on the bungee platform.

Bungee jumping in the rainforest just outside of Cairns between Christmas and New Year was metaphorical for the fact that I'd ended up in Japan in the first place. I didn't give it a lot of thought. My thought process was as follows:

We are in Australia. This is the place to bungee jump. If it were dangerous, this company wouldn't be in operation. Ken can't do it. I might as well.

Completely rational!

I didn't do much research into who I was putting in charge of my life. But I did look into the company enough to see that they were *the* gold standard for bungee jumping, not only in Australia but around the world, and I decided to go for it. I wasn't at all fazed at the thought that it could end up being disastrous.

On the day of the jump, Tomoko came with me. The rest went shopping and exploring around town. The site, which still operates today, is a short drive outside of Cairns, and the jump takes place over a beautiful gorge in the thick, lush rainforest. As the young men strapped my ankles in, they asked me my weight (ugh) because they had to adjust the equipment according to my weight, height, and how far down I wanted to go. They also asked if I wanted to touch the water (there was a river running through the gorge), and I declined. Here is where I was a bit cautious—I figured if I said no, then if, by accident, I did touch the water, hopefully I wouldn't be going down so far as to crack my head on a rock in the river or something. I obviously wasn't being logical enough to recognize that the chances were likely quite high that they had already inspected the river below the bungee platform for rocks, subsequently removing any rocks that could crack a jumper's head open.

I was set. And by the time they had me strapped in and ready to jump, I was really excited. Standing on top of the platform, 100 meters above the river, I looked out onto the ocean where the Great Barrier Reef was and across the top of the rainforest. Even though the day was a bit overcast, the view was spectacular, and the thought of what I was about to do suddenly exhilarated me. I was pumped! Until I looked ... not across ... but down. And then I freaked out.

What was I thinking? What am I doing? This is not a smart idea! I said to myself all within less than a split second. But it was too late. The young men who had strapped me in were looking at the camera (I got a nice VHS tape souvenir of this event) and yelling, "IT'S LONNER, THE WILD BULL RIDER FROM CANADER! FIVE ... FOUR ... THREE ..."

There was no backing out. I shut off my brain and ... STEPPED ... not jumped ... off the platform and promptly proceeded to scream my face off as I have never screamed before. You would have thought I was being violently murdered.

The free fall was terrifying, but after the split second in which I had concluded I was going to die, I suddenly felt the gentle tug of the bungee cord as I slowed down and started to swing back up. The bounce back down wasn't nearly as fast or as far, and by the time I had stopped bouncing, I was saying to myself, *That's it? It's over already?* After the initial free fall, the rest of the "jump" was incredibly fun … except for the few moments when I was hanging upside down waiting for the men at the bottom to come in their raft and release me. All the blood rushing to my head made me feel again like my head was going to explode. But release me they did. I flopped into the raft, my ankles still bound together, and answered the guys above, who yelled down at me, "How was that?" with two enthusiastic thumbs up.

Like my move to Japan, disaster did not ensue, and I added one more item to my list of things I have done in life that when I look at now, I think, *What was I thinking?!?* But that's the point: do this stuff while you're young—before you get older and overly cautious. And smart.

When I got back onto dry land, Tomoko asked how it was.

"Great!" I said, "SO much fun! But I will NEVER do that again!!"

The End of a Vacation, the End of a Year

On the one day in Australia that Ken wasn't scuba diving, our entire entourage went whitewater rafting. Most of us had never attempted this mode of transportation before, but we were all game to give it a try.

Our guide, a fun-loving young Aboriginal man, quickly realized he had a group of adventure-seeking tourists on his hands. Consequently, he took us over the sections of the river—such as the appropriately named Full Stop Drop, Helicopter, Satan's Toilet Bowl, and Zig Zag—backwards, forwards, sideways, full speed. In certain sections, he guided our raft over the roughest, steepest drops instead of the easier, safer options, and we ate it up. Our guide also purposely flipped us over when going over some of the rapids (because he knew we would love it). The only mishap of the day happened when we got back into the raft after the lunch break. A guide from another raft, while cruising past us, looked at Michelle No. 2 and informed her in his charming Aussie accent, "Excuse me, ma'am. You've got your helmet on backwards." After laughing heartily, she corrected her helmet, and we carried on and finished a memorable, exhilarating day.

But there was one more adventure left to conquer before flying back north.

日本

I can't swim. Well, I can, but I'm not a great swimmer and a timid one at that, so in my mind I can't swim.

As any mother does, mine put me into swimming lessons when I was a kid, and it took me not one, not two, but three tries to pass the beginning level. I think it had something to do with the fact that I was five when the movie *Jaws* came out, and although I was under strict instructions to go to bed while my parents were watching it on TV, I snuck out of my room and hid behind my dad's recliner while they were watching it. Well, I lasted only a few minutes. The opening scene had me utterly horrified, and after the poor woman was dissected by the shark, I snuck back to bed. It was right around then that my fear of the bathtub settled into place. Every time I took a bath, I was paranoid that a shark was going to come up the drain of the bathtub and attack me in the same way that the woman in the movie was massacred.

Anyway, I finally passed my first level of swimming lessons, so of course, my mom promptly registered me in the next level, starting the following week. Part of the curriculum in the second level required us to tread water in the diving tank for a certain period of time. Treading water in the main pool was bad enough, (I utterly hated the whole swimming lessons experience—every aspect of it), but at least I could put my feet on the bottom of the pool if I started to panic. Not so in the diving tank, and about halfway through the second lesson of my new level, I was trying to tread water in the diving tank but lost my momentum and starting to sink.

Down. Down. Down. Of course, I panicked, so while I was thrashing and splashing and gulping, thankfully my instructor noticed my predicament and pulled me up, out of the water onto the deck beside the pool. By then, I had swallowed a fair bit of awful-tasting pool water, my nose was bleeding, and I was utterly terrified. That was the last swim lesson I attended. I put my foot down after that. On solid ground.

When our group decided to head to Australia, I decided I needed to conquer my dread of water so I could at least catch a glimpse of some of the reef. I convinced Ken to give me a few informal lessons in a local pool roughly halfway between his apartment and mine. He kindly showed me a few tips and guided me to the point where I was comfortable doing the breaststroke and side stroke, and I was able to tread water for several minutes without panicking. My confidence was building. I felt like I had a bit of a base to work with if I decided to venture into the ocean in the land "down undah."

Our travelling group headed to Green Island, off the coast of Cairns, for a day excursion. Swimsuits in tow, we took the forty-five-minute ferry ride to the island and settled in to enjoy the day. Ken was scuba diving daily, and in the evenings he was telling us about his dives with sharks, turtles, and a plethora of other marine life. By the time the rest of us donned our life jackets to get into the water and explore the reef, we were anxious to see some of what he was seeing every day.

Feeling a bit more confident in my pseudo-swimming abilities, I put my faith in my life jacket, strapping a snorkel mask onto my face and flippers onto my feet. As a prairie girl, I hadn't had much experience near oceans up to that point. The beach near my home in Japan wasn't one where people did much swimming. Most people hung out on the beach or went for walks or bike rides along the shore. So I was pleasantly surprised at the buoyancy of my body in the salty water.

In mere moments, I settled into floating comfortably and fearlessly on the ocean's surface, keeping my head in the water and checking out the life below me. Knowing I wasn't in any immediate danger of drowning, thanks to the support of the life jacket and the buoyancy of salt water, I was able to enjoy an extended period of time in the water, snorkelling and exploring. In fact, I thoroughly enjoyed the experience and wasn't the least bit afraid until I started to drift out a little farther than I wanted to. No matter; I swam a bit closer to shore and continued to enjoy my first time snorkelling.

Turns out I had enjoyed myself a bit too much. My swimsuit's scooped back had exposed much of my own. Because I had forgotten to put sunscreen on my back, it was covered in water blisters the next day. Despite how painful it was to wear not only a shirt but especially a bra, I spared my travel companions the horror of seeing me without either, suffering through the next few days until my back started to heal.

That day, I discovered a new favourite activity. I had never imagined myself being comfortable—much less enjoying myself—in the water. I enjoy canoeing and kayaking, but until that day in Oz, my fear of water had prevented me from ever enjoying being IN water deeper than three or four feet. I have since had the opportunity to snorkel in the Red Sea and also in the Caribbean, where I followed a sea turtle around for about twenty minutes. The underwater world is magical.

日本

I checked off every adventurous option in the area that appealed to me—snorkelling the Great Barrier Reef, bungee jumping, whitewater rafting, and eating a python dinner at the local exotic restaurant. We returned to Japan, where we would still have a few days off before work started again (January 4 for Ken, January 5 for the rest of us). We flew back to Tōkyō on December 31, and we were all home in our apartments before the calendar flipped over to the new year.

日本

New Year's Day 1993, I woke up back at my apartment in Japan with another horrible sinus headache and was completely stuffed up again. OK. This wasn't a cold. Obviously, something in Japan was making me sick. Extremely sick.

I had no food in the house since we had been gone for ten days, and I also had no money since I had exchanged all of my cash into Aussie dollars. Sick as I was, I needed groceries, so I headed out to the bank so I could hit up the grocery store.

No go. The bank machines were closed, and I never even made it to the grocery store since I had no money. No matter. I had some noodles and canned goods I could eat until the next day. Of *course* businesses were closed; it was New Year's Day—one of the most significant holidays on the Japanese calendar. Silly me. (By this time, I had been in Japan long enough that I knew bank machines were closed overnight and on national holidays, too.) I decided to wait and try again the next day.

January 2. Sick and stuffed up still. Ugh. Up and out of bed, showered, and dressed. I waited until late morning when I was sure the bank machines would be operational again and grocery stores would be open.

Nope. Still no response from the ATM.

Huh. That was weird.

I tried on January 3—again, to no avail.

Turns out, not only were all stores and businesses closed January 1–4 for the national holidays, but so were the bank machines. I made a mental note to myself: *Next year, make sure I have enough cash on hand by December 31 to get me through till January 4. No, wait. No need for cash since nothing is open. Instead, just make sure there is enough food in the fridge or cupboard for four days.*

By January 4, I was tired of crackers and hungry enough to finish the rest of that two-kilo steak.

I'm Allergic to Japan!

My constant breathing problems became a huge source of distress. I had no idea what the problem was, so I asked the manager of my school to make an appointment for me with an ear, nose, and throat specialist. (I still wasn't fluent enough to find or make an appointment with such a specialist myself. Our managers helped us with these sorts of tasks!) I had toughed it out for a couple of weeks after returning from Australia, but I just wasn't able to shake whatever was ailing me. As healthy as I had been down under, something in Japan was obviously making me ill. I had never had a health problem like this before, and I started to fear that if I couldn't get it resolved, I would have no choice but to resign from my job and move back to Canada. I had signed on for two years but fully intended to stay for at least three, possibly up to five. The thought of having to go home after one year in Japan, right when I was feeling like I was finding my groove, was really upsetting.

One of my lovely students from my daytime housewife class graciously took me to the doctor's appointment. Keiko was a wonderful woman in her forties—the type of woman who is always smiling and would drop anything if she could help someone in need. She did just that for me, and I will always be grateful to her for accompanying me to the appointment. Although my language skills were rapidly and steadily improving, talking to a doctor was well beyond the scope of my ability. And, after all, this was my health; I didn't want to leave any room for errors or misunderstandings. She translated for me during the appointment, took me to the pharmacy (where she also translated between me and the pharmacist), and then drove me home with my new meds. The fact that she drove me to the doctor's office, the pharmacy, and then home in a brand-new silver Mercedes made me a little more comfortable, as well.

Turns out I *was* allergic to Japan. The specialist tested me and for the first time, I was diagnosed with allergies. To what, I still didn't know, but it was all starting to make sense now. I was living in a humid climate, so something in the difference between coastal Japan and dry Alberta was making me sick. (I did a full round of allergy tests when I moved back to Canada and the results showed that I'm allergic to a few things, including budgies, but the main culprit was and is dust mites.)

The specialist prescribed a generic-looking white pill that turned out to be completely magical. As per the translation Keiko offered, I was apparently to take this pill once a day every day. Forever. I took the first one, and within a couple of hours, I was as good as gold. And I stayed that way for almost a week. Whoa. Magic pill indeed. I'm not a big fan of taking medication. I do so only when necessary—and, oddly, my body reacts strongly to medicine, so I typically don't need as high of a dose or as long of a prescription as most people. I can actually feel my body recovering within a couple of hours of taking antibiotics, which are supposed to take three to five days to kick in.

And there it was. I didn't have to leave Japan after all, but I was destined to take this medication for the remainder of my time in Japan. This white pill seemed to be the only way to control the allergies I had developed in my first eight to nine months in the country. Instead of taking the pills every day, though, I took them as needed, and over the next two years, there were stints when I didn't need them for several weeks at a time. When I returned to Canada, I asked a pharmacist in my hometown about these pills. Turns out they were a steroid that had not been approved for use in Canada. Eek. But they had worked and allowed me to remain in Japan.

With the solution in hand, I settled back into sticking to my plan to stay in Japan for at least three years. At this point, I was coming up to the end of year one, and with a national holiday falling on a Saturday in March,[33] I had a three-day weekend coming up. What better way to commemorate my one-year anniversary than to take a long-weekend trip to Seoul, South Korea, with Michelle No. 1 and Brian.

---

[33] National holidays in Japan are set by date, not by day of the week as they are in Canada or the US. Instead of a holiday being on the first Monday of the month, for example, the holiday is on the same date every year, so each year, the day off would land on a different day of the week. I appreciated this. It was nice to have mid-week breaks sometimes, but in March of 1993, and then again in November, these holidays resulted in my getting long weekends.

It's Your Party, You Can Puke If You Want To. Just Don't Do It on Me!

Michelle arranged to meet me and Brian at Narita Airport. Since Brian lived in Tōkyō, he and I arranged to meet at one the city's main train stations, where I had to change trains anyway to get to the airport. We had no problem finding each other this time. We met up on the platform of the train we needed to board and waited for our train.

He looked horrible. Before the train came, he fessed up that he had been up drinking all night with a friend and had come to the train station on zero sleep, somewhere between still drunk and hungover. And he was kinda stinky. *OK, whatever. Your problem, buddy. It's your own fault that you're going to feel awful for the rest of this day*, I thought. He got no sympathy from me.

I shrugged it off and we got on the train.

Two hours later, we arrived at Narita, found Michelle, and checked in for our flights. The whole process was seamless. We went through security and made our way to the general area of the gate, where Brian announced he was hungry.

Well, I was hungry by this time, too, since breakfast had been several hours prior, so the three of us found something to eat. Brian's choice was spaghetti carbonara and a small carton of milk. I don't remember what Michelle or I had. (Yes, that's definitely foreshadowing. Insert dramatic music here …)

Our flight was on schedule, so we boarded and got settled in our seats. I was in the window seat, Brian was beside me, and Michelle was on the other side of him across the aisle. La la la, everything was normal and fine and dandy until the plane slllloooooowwwwwlllllyyyy started backing away from the gate.

Suddenly, Brian's elbow was repeatedly and quickly jabbing my ribs, and he was motioning to the pocket in the seatback in front of me, telling me to get a puke bag out for him. I quickly grabbed it as he also grabbed the one in front of him, and he let loose. I immediately started hitting the call button repeatedly as hard as I could, as if pounding on it would make the flight attendant come more quickly. He filled both bags, but in the process of changing bags, he also missed, projectile vomiting all over the seatback in front of me and on my right leg. IT SMELLED AWFUL. I mean, puke never smells good, but ... alcohol that had been churning in stomach acid for hours, mixed with now-curdled milk and spaghetti carbonara. It was all I could do to keep my own lunch down.

The flight attendant came by just as Brian finished barfing and told us that since we were now approaching the runway, we couldn't leave our seats to go to the bathroom to clean up. I asked her if she could bring me something to wipe the tray and the seat in front of me and a minute later, she came back with ... a wool blanket. Not helpful.

By now I was disgusted with both Brian and the flight attendant, resignedly wiping the dangling pieces of spaghetti off the tray on the seatback in front of me. I handed the blanket to Brian, slumped over in my seat, and stared out the window for the entire two-hour flight. I was so furious with him; I couldn't tear my eyes away from the non-view out the window during the whole flight.

We arrived in Seoul and breezed through customs. We all figured it was likely because Brian and I both smelled so bad that the poor customs officer just wanted to get rid of us.

By this time, I was developing a massive headache (maybe I'm allergic to stinky, boozy puke, too). A cab driver dropped us off at our hotel and we grabbed the room the three of us were sharing. I took my glasses off, put them on the end table, and flopped down on one of the beds to rest with my arm over my eyes. I was still livid, and I still wasn't speaking to Brian. The headache was a good excuse to take a bit more time to try and let go of my anger.

Brian had another problem. We were only in Korea for a three-day weekend, so we had all packed light, only bringing carry-on luggage. Brian, however, had brought less than that. He had brought a couple of shirts, but no extra pants. The only pants he had were the jeans he was wearing, which he had also spattered with puke. I had a change of pants, but his pants and mine stunk so badly, we immediately decided to use the hotel laundry service to get them washed.

Michelle to the rescue. She lent Brian a pair of super roomy, flowy, lightweight sweatpants-style tapered leggings since his jeans were headed to the hotel laundry room. He changed into Michelle's ladies' Aladdin pants. I had changed into my clean jeans, and Brian took it upon himself to call the front desk to arrange to have someone pick up our laundry.

As I was laying on the bed with my arms covering my eyes, I could, of course, only hear his side of the conversation.

"Hello. We have some pants we would like to send to the laundry service. Could someone come to get our pants?"

Pause.

"Some pants. We would like to send our pants to the laundry. We need them cleaned as soon as possible."

Pause.

"Pants. Pants."

Pause.

"Yes, pants."

Pause.

"Thank you."

Click.

"They're sending someone up right away to get our laundry," Brian informed me and Michelle.

Excellent. Let's get these smelly things out of our room and move past this incident so we can enjoy what little time we have in Seoul.

Brian picked up the plastic bag we had put our laundry in and waited. Sure enough, moments later, there was a knock on the door.

I didn't hear any speaking. All I heard was the door quickly open and then close, and after it closed, I heard Brian burst out laughing. What the heck was going on?

I removed my arm from my eyes and opened them up. My vision is terrible, so all I could see was the outline of Brian standing at the foot of the bed with one of his arms slightly raised, looking in my direction. I reached over, grabbed my glasses, and put them on.

Indeed, there was Brian, standing there, looking at me, laughing his head off, and holding up a pen.

It took a second for my brain to register the fact that the person at the front desk must not speak English well enough to have understood what Brian had said. Yep. Brian had opened the door to see a Korean man standing there, who shoved a pen at Brian and promptly walked away before Brian could give him our pants or even say anything.

By this time, my Tylenol was taking effect. The misunderstanding with the front desk clerk was exactly what needed to happen to break the tension that had been hanging between me and Brian since he barfed all over me and our side of the airplane. I couldn't help but laugh.

Since I was feeling better and we were settled into our room, we decided to head out to explore the area. There was still the issue of the putrid pants, though.

"Well, once we get to the front desk, if we put our stinky pants on the counter, surely they will figure out that we want them to do laundry service," I suggested.

When we got downstairs, we put Brian's and my jeans on the counter and pointed at the puke stains. The front desk clerk crinkled his nose—a sure sign that he got our meaning—and he nodded, assuring us that he understood our request. We left the hotel to do a bit of sightseeing and to find a place to have our first Korean meal, with Brian looking ridiculous in the genie-like women's flowy sweatpants.

A Real Watch

Shopping in Korea was a different experience than it was in Japan. There is no bartering in Japan, but in most other Asian countries, bartering with street vendors or in markets is common and even expected. And these street vendors sell a lot of knock-offs.

We didn't do much shopping, but we did check out the street vendors, who sold a variety of items. I had heard before heading to

Korea that Seoul was a great place to pick up a leather jacket for a reasonable price. Having never owned a leather jacket before, I kept my eyes open for one. I found a heavy green one that I fell in love with. I ended up wearing it to death until it practically fell apart more than ten years later. I definitely got my money's worth out of that jacket, and I loved it—it was unique, comfortable, warm, and useful with the large pockets inside and out.

None of us was in the market for anything else except for Michelle, who said she needed a new watch. Brian and I waited patiently while she bartered with a street vendor, haggling over what was no more than the equivalent of a couple of dollars on the price of the watch, even though it was cheap to begin with. Michelle wouldn't cave; she drove a hard bargain. She really wanted the watch, but she wasn't going to "overpay." As she haggled and argued over the trivial amount, Brian injected himself into the interaction, reminding her, "It's not a real Gucci!" to which she responded, "Yeah, but it's a real watch!" She wanted it, and she finally got it for a satisfactory price (about C$20 instead of C$25).

At the end of our second day, which we also spent touring and shopping, we were pleased to return to our hotel room to find that my and Brian's jeans had been laundered and returned. I was fine still wearing my second pair, but Brian was happy to get out of Michelle's magic-carpet pants and return them to her. We were all happy for the puke stench to be a thing of the past.

The trip to Seoul was quick but it was a nice weekend getaway—a change of scenery from the dreariness at the end of March and beginning of April in Japan. We headed back right before cherry blossom season, which is tied with autumn as the most stunning time of year. (Autumn—with its wild oranges, yellows, and reds of the leaves on the trees—is also beautiful.)

CHAPTER 6

PEOPLE MAKE THE PLACE

Baking Carrot Biscuits

The core group of friends that I had made during my first year in Japan became my main social group. In addition to the trip to Australia we had all taken together, some of us travelled together to different destinations.

Five of us went to Saipan, the tiny (although largest) island in the US Commonwealth of the Northern Mariana Islands, for a few days of sunshine and beach time. While there, I rode a Jet Ski for the first time. I also tried "windsurfing," if that's what you could call my attempts. Windsurfing takes a lot of upper-body strength and balance, and I am greatly lacking in both. I averaged about two seconds of standing upright and holding onto the sail before pitching into the ocean even though there was barely a mild breeze on the day I attempted this sport. After repeatedly falling and getting back up, I eventually got frustrated and gave up, deciding windsurfing was definitely not for me.

On the way back from Saipan, the unknowing person working the desk when we checked in for our flights back to Tōkyō decided for some reason that we all needed a free upgrade to business class. Well, none of us had ever flown anything other than economy. So, of course, we acted like bratty children for the entire flight, playing with the pillows, giggling at all of the food and drinks we were getting, and mucking around with the seats checking out the extra legroom. I'm sure the people who actually paid for business class appreciated us.

One of the members of my core group, Teresa, was a fun-loving, gregarious girl from Oregon and someone that I felt a kinship with, a bit more so than some of the others. We seemed to be more like-minded and have more in common than the others, and we are still friends today.

Teresa's apartment in Japan was bigger than most; it was roughly the same size as mine but was divided into separate rooms, and the layout was more like a typical apartment you would see in Canada or the US. The kitchen, living room, and bedroom were all separate rooms. The size and layout of her pad, along with the fact that her apartment was between where I and Ken lived, meant that her apartment, by default, became the party house. Her apartment was where I, and sometimes one or two others, would crash if we missed the last train. Another teacher also lived in the same building as Teresa, but she was living there with her boyfriend, so Teresa had more room for strays. Because we all worked late and therefore started our workday late, we were used to staying up until the wee hours. So when we missed the last train, if we weren't out racing around the go-kart track or playing pool or singing karaoke, we would often be just hanging out at Teresa's apartment listening to music. We all loved Queen, so putting

Queen's *Greatest Hits* CD in the CD player immediately when we all gathered in Teresa's apartment became an unspoken rule. We would sit around on the floor playing cards, laughing, and singing at the top of our lungs for hours.

One night, we caught Ken singing the wrong lyrics to one of the songs, and an argument ensued. He insisted that what he was singing was correct; Teresa and I insisted we were right. We played the song over and over, but we never did convince him that his wacky lyrics were wrong (they were). Well, this ended up spawning a game of Misheard Lyrics. We took turns going around the circle, belting out the wrong lyrics to songs and seeing how quickly one of the others could guess the song and what the correct lyric was. Now, roughly three decades later, I still can't listen to certain songs without singing "Baking Carrot Biscuits" ("Taking Care of Business") or "Living on Toast and Jam" ("Tulsa Time") at the top of my lungs with a wide smile. Those, and the Queen songs, consistently make me break out in a big grin as I remember those fun nights.

Teresa was our Irish representative, so every St. Patrick's Day, regardless of which day of the week it fell on, we were required to go out and celebrate with her. We all followed her lead because it was "her" holiday, so the rule was that we would do whatever she decided. St. Patrick's Day never fell on a weekend while I was living in Japan, so each year, I ended up crashing at her apartment and then catching the train home in the morning with plenty of time to get ready for work.

I hadn't yet met Teresa on my first St. Patrick's Day in Japan since it was two weeks after I arrived, but in my second year, I joined in the festivities. Teresa brought green food colouring to the party. Several of us were at an izakaya in her city having drinks and lots of food. I started the evening with red wine because that's what I felt like drinking. Teresa brought the green food colouring out of her purse and proceeded to put a few drops of it into everyone's beer. After drinking two glasses of wine, I was made to switch to beer so that I could have green beer and thereby properly celebrate St. Patrick's Day with my friend. Because I am a good friend, I complied, and the celebrations continued.

At the end of the party, we all went our separate ways. Because Michelle No. 2 and I were crashing at Teresa's apartment, one of Teresa's students, who had been with us all evening, was our driver. He drove me, Teresa, Michelle, and the other teacher from Teresa's building back to their apartment building. I was in the back seat between Michelle and the other teacher. Teresa was in the front giving her student directions.

Suddenly, when we were roughly halfway back to the apartment building, I wasn't feeling well. I knew I was going to throw up. The student couldn't stop as there was nowhere to pull over. Panic ensued. Michelle and the other teacher quickly looked around the back seat of the car. The student's English textbooks were in a white plastic bag behind my head, so my friends quickly grabbed the bag, yanked the books out of it, and handed it to me. I cleanly threw up into the bag and then held on to it tightly, keeping it closed while we continued to Teresa's apartment.

When we arrived, we all got out of the car. What to do with the bag? There was a garbage bin on the corner of the street, and as was the case 100 per cent of the time, the garbage bin was overflowing. (Honestly, in my entire three years in Japan, I don't recall ever seeing a public garbage bin that wasn't overflowing.) I shrugged my shoulders, plopped the bag on top of the mound of garbage, and followed the others into the apartment building while the bag opened and let off some steam.

I've not been able to bring myself to drink green beer since.

Once More with Feeling

A little-known fact about me: I can play the *shamisen*. Well, I can play one song on the shamisen. But that counts, right?

A shamisen is the three-stringed instrument heard in traditional Japanese music. Its body is like that of a banjo but is square rather than round. The instrument has a long, thin neck, which makes playing easier for someone like me who has small hands. Like a violin, the shamisen has no marked frets, so figuring out where to place your left fingers on the neck to hit the correct notes is the biggest challenge. The right hand picks the strings with a *bachi*, a large (usually wooden) pick that looks somewhat like a spatula. For someone who plays guitar (or probably any stringed instrument), learning shamisen is not a terribly difficult jump.

Tomoko had been studying tea ceremony for several years. One Sunday afternoon around six months after I arrived in Japan, she invited me to her home so she could perform a tea ceremony for me. When I arrived, I saw that I would be taking part in the ceremony with another Canadian I hadn't met yet. Mark was from Windsor, Ontario. He lived and taught in a school (not affiliated with my company) in Zengyō, an area of Fujisawa one train stop further up the line from where I lived. He didn't know any other expats, so I invited him along the next time our little group was getting together. He quickly became part of our gang.

In our first conversation, I learned that Mark, like me, played guitar. He had also gotten himself into a weekly arrangement to learn shamisen. His teacher, Mrs. Beppu (or, more appropriately, Beppu-*sensei*[34]) was an elderly widowed woman who owned some of the

---

[34] Sensei: In English, sensei translates to teacher but more so means master. It is used for not only schoolteachers but anyone who is a master of a certain

hospitals in Fujisawa. She was heavily involved in the arts scene and was well-connected to local politicians and other dignitaries. Word got back to her that Mark had a new Canadian friend who was also musically inclined, and I was invited to join the shamisen lessons.

Beppu-sensei gifted Mark and me each our own bachi that we could take home with us, but we were under strict instructions to bring them every Monday to our lesson. Sadly, we were not gifted the shamisen (they cost well over C$1,000 each and many are worth several thousand dollars), but she had quite an extensive collection of them and designated one of them to Mark and one to me every week.

Mark had had several lessons by the time I joined, but he wasn't terribly far ahead of me, and it didn't take me long to catch on and catch up. Beppu-sensei was teaching us a song called "Matsu no Midori" (translated as "The Green Pine"), a centuries-old, widely-known traditional song whose lyrics describe a geisha named Midori walking among the pine trees in the spring.[35] I quickly learned to read the sheet music and place my fingers on the neck to hit the notes. Beppu-sensei had kindly put marked tape along the top of the neck to show us where the frets were located. I quickly fell in love with this lightweight, simplistic looking and sounding instrument.

Japanese learning goes deep, not wide. To the Japanese, learning a skill means perfecting it. A lot of repetition ensures that the task is performed correctly, precisely, and respectfully. Sushi chefs train for upwards of ten years before they are considered masters. Likewise, Tomoko had been studying tea ceremony for several years and still considered herself an apprentice. It was this approach that our

---

skill, such as martial arts, flower arrangement, or other arts. Sensei is also used to address doctors, lawyers, etc., as a term of high respect for people in those roles.

[35] komuso.com/pieces/pieces.pl?piece=3939

shamisen teacher took in teaching us to master one song and one song only. She started us by working on the first section of the song over and over, and it was weeks before we moved on to the whole song.

Monday after Monday, we showed up for 10 a.m. lessons. Mark and I dutifully sat *seiza*[36] on the tatami during our lesson. Whenever our teacher left the room to use the bathroom or take a phone call, we would quickly take a break, adjust our legs, and sit cross-legged or even stand for a few minutes. When we heard her coming back, we'd quickly scuttle back into seiza. She fed us lunch every Monday as well, and lunch was beef curry. Every Monday. Her meal schedule was the same as that of the hospital she lived above, so we ate the same food that patients in the hospital got ... and it was delicious!

After learning the same bars of music week after week, Mark and I started having the same conversation every time she left the room: When would we get to try a new song? We thought it was bizarre, hilarious, and a bit annoying that she had us working on the same section of the same song week after week. We had yet to figure out that the answer was "never." In keeping with tradition, she wanted us to go deep with the one song and master it rather than do a mediocre job of learning two, three, or more songs. To me, this was an interesting cultural difference and one that was frustrating, even though I consider myself a perfectionist. Of course, in the land of treating your sensei with the utmost respect, we never did find the courage to ask, even politely, if we could try a second song.

---

[36] Seiza: Traditional Japanese seated position with the front of your lower legs flat on the ground and your bum resting on your heels. Most foreigners sitting seiza for the first few times find their legs and feet falling asleep within a few minutes, but with practice, one can comfortably maintain seiza position for more than thirty minutes.

After a few months, we discovered the other reason she wanted us to master the one song. Fujisawa is a sister city of Windsor, Ontario, and the two cities have a strong connection. That was, in fact, how Mark had gotten his teaching job in Fujisawa: he was from Windsor and knew somebody who knew somebody. And now, about six months into our shamisen lessons, through our stilted conversations with our teacher who knew only a handful of English words, she informed us of her plans. She had scheduled us to perform our song for a group of officials in government and the arts from both Windsor and Fujisawa when a ballet group and some other representatives from Windsor were to visit in a few weeks.

GULP! OK, maybe we DIDN'T need to move on to a second song after all. Suddenly, the pressure of performing in front of an actual audience made our attention to this one song more urgent. Japan is a culture of history, ritual, symbolism, respect, and even more respect. For us to butcher one of their traditional songs on one of their national instruments in front of local dignitaries would be utterly shameful.

And then there was the age-old sentiment: "But I haven't got a thing to wear!" Performing this song in a formal Japanese setting in even formal western clothes was out of the question. Out came the tape measure. Sensei had her housemaid measure Mark and me from top to bottom, around the middle, upside down, inside out. Two weeks later, she gave us each a package during our lesson. She had had custom (and matching!) *yukata*[37] made for each of us, and even though we were both dreading our performance, the yukata were special and

---

[37] Yukata: a less formal style of kimono, usually made of cotton instead of silk. Yukata are worn in the summer when it is hot since they are cooler than a heavy kimono. Both men and women wear yukata.

meaningful gifts. I still have mine, although I don't have much occasion to wear it in southern Alberta.

Well, this was all incentive enough to take our lessons much more seriously. Our honour, and that of our teacher, was on the line—and, as most people know, honour is a pretty big deal in Japan. The importance of making our teacher look good was not lost on us. I didn't care about saving face for myself, but even though I was living in Japan, I was still a "guest" in this culture and I wanted to show respect. We attacked that damn song with great attentiveness every Monday from that point on, earning our curry in the process.

The Windsorites arrived. The day had come, and I was dreading it. I wanted to crawl under the tatami mats, never to be seen again. We donned our yukata (with some help) and put on our best smiles, bowing to the Japanese dignitaries, shaking hands with those from Canada. I doubly wanted to be on my best behaviour—not only were we representing our teacher, but the international visitors were from my country and Mark's hometown. I felt the pressure of not making a doofus of myself so *no one* would lose face.

Our performance was painful. Not physically painful. By this time, Mark and I had both acquired appropriate callouses on our left fingers, and we had spent enough time in seiza that to remain in that position for the five-minute song was nothing to blink at. BUT I WAS SO NERVOUS! Truth is, we performed the song almost flawlessly. But to sit seiza in a custom-made yukata in a room full of Japanese and Canadian strangers, many of whom were prestigious in the arts scene in both countries, playing a song that every Japanese person in the room knew well. That was as nerve-racking as it gets for this introverted, small-town farm girl who would rather be on a mountain in hiking boots or on the back of a horse in jeans and cowboy boots. But play we did.

Pling—pling—pling—pling—pling—pling—pling—pling—pling—pling—pling—pling—pling ...

We picked and plucked for several minutes along with our teacher, and the entire crowd went wild. The Canadians were dumbfounded, and the Japanese people were honoured that *we* had honoured them by learning and performing this piece of their culture. In the end, it was a ton of fun. I was happy to have made our teacher proud of us—and proud of herself—for having turned these two Canadians into people who could embrace and show respect to her ancient culture. She reveled in showing us off. We were the hit of the party. The smiles and bows came a lot more naturally to me, Mark, and the Japanese attendees for the rest of the day.

日本

A couple of years ago, I was in a Japanese restaurant in Summerlin, a suburb of Las Vegas, enjoying one of the most authentic and delicious Japanese meals I've had outside of Japan. Minutes after I came back from the bathroom, I squealed with delight and felt *natsukashii*[38] when "Matsu no Midori" suddenly came over the speakers. I had to stop eating, sit back, and let the warm feeling of nostalgia wash over me while my dining companion looked at me and waited for me to tell her the reason for the big smile on my face.

---

[38] Natsukashii: the feeling of nostalgia, but deeper than that—a longing and a fondness for something meaningful and heartwarming from the past. It encompasses joy and gratitude for an experience that you know you will never have again.

Tobogganing on Tanzawa

Within a couple of weeks of meeting Mark, I introduced him to the rest of my circle of friends, and he became part of our group. But outside of the shamisen lessons, he and I also spent time together without the rest of the gang. This was partly because we had a lot of common interests, partly because we had the same days off, and partly because we lived a few minutes from each other. (Nearly everyone else lived about thirty minutes away.) One of our common loves was hiking.

Japan is a great country to move to if you love hiking. When my company had asked me if I had a preference of where I would want to live, I simply said I wanted to be somewhere that I could do some good hiking. That pretty much covers most of the country, and when I found out where I was placed, I was pleased to be getting "the best of both worlds"—or three, really. I was close enough to Tōkyō that I could go to the city for a day or even half a day for shopping or sightseeing. I was a thirty-minute train ride (and later, after I bought my bike, a thirty-minute bicycle ride) from the beach. And there were mountains in every direction except south, the direction of the ocean.

Mark and I lived close enough to several great outdoor opportunities, and we went on day trips now and then to various hiking spots. One of the hikes we both really wanted to do was a day trip to the top of Mount Tanzawa, a short train ride north of where we lived. In late-January 1993, we made a plan to conquer Mount Tanzawa and set out a few days later to do so.

The area where we lived was quite mild in the winters compared to the Canadian prairies. The temperature never got below freezing; on most winter days, the temperature was slightly above. Fujisawa got a small skiff of snow maybe a couple of times per year, but it usually melted by midday. There was more snow farther inland—and, of course, on the mountains—but Tanzawa is only 1,567 meters high. Mild winter conditions meant Tanzawa could be hiked at any time of the year even though there might be a bit of snow on it. The day we chose was mild for January, and with solid hiking boots, hiking pants, and proper jackets, we had no reason to worry about the elements.

Because the mountain wasn't terribly high, we plodded along, one foot in front of the other, and made it to the top in a couple of hours without too much effort. Snow blanketed the higher portions of the trail, but it wasn't very deep and didn't present any hazards. The hike was a moderate climb on a sunny, comfortable winter day. We were appropriately dressed and had brought food along, so we enjoyed a lunch stop at the top of the mountain once we had summited.

It was turning out to be a perfect hike until we started to descend in the afternoon. Naturally, the day had warmed up, so the snow was beginning to melt. The trail was a little icy in some spots, but more than anything, it was slushy, sloppy, and slippery. Because Tanzawa is close to a lot of towns and cities and it's not terribly difficult, it's a popular hike. As we descended, a lot of people were coming up. In particular, we noticed a lot of well-dressed women in their thirties to fifties for some reason—maybe because it was a Monday and a lot of women who did not work were out for a social event.

As we continued hiking down, the trail got so slippery and the snow so slushy that I fell a few times. Mark was getting a little frustrated, as well. Finally, after battling to stay on our feet, we looked at each other and shrugged our shoulders. Without saying a word, I flopped down on my butt and proceeded to slide down the mountain. Mark followed suit, and so we descended, laughing and shrieking the whole way while sliding down the slushy trail.

As we suspected, sliding down the mountain on our behinds was easier than trying to hike down. All of the middle-aged Japanese women must have been terrified at these loud, rambunctious twenty-three-year-old Canadians bum-sliding down a mountain toward them, and indeed, we did get some funny looks. By the halfway mark, the slush vanished. The rest of the path was mud or just dry dirt, so we stood up and hiked the rest of the day. While sliding, we had, of course, encountered some patches of ice, slush, water, and mud, so we were completely covered from bum to heel in mud. By the time we got to the train station, though, the mud all over our legs and butts had dried a fair bit. We plopped on the train seats and headed home, feeling accomplished for having conquered the mountain.

Monster Chicken

Carlos came blasting into our lives like the little human hurricane he was.

Peruvian by citizenship, his ethnicity was half Japanese, half Latino. Because of his Japanese heritage, he had moved from Peru to Japan in search of himself but also for a more stable income and a better life overall. He was energetic, loud, wacky, hilarious, and tiny. We often joked among ourselves that if he wore overalls, he would have been a dead ringer for the lead singer of Dexys Midnight Runners. Carlos was a bundle of energy and positivity who came out of nowhere. (Well, technically, another member of our group had met him at Aikido[39] lessons, and, as I did with Mark, brought him into our group.) He quickly became an energetic and fun presence in our social outings.

---

[39] Aikido: a Japanese martial art. The techniques derive from samurai fighting moves, and the modern practice of Aikido focuses on developing individual discipline, wisdom, and harmony rather than competition with another person.

Carlos had a big heart and was always wanting to learn about Canadian and American culture while sharing his cultures with us. On one occasion, he offered to cook Peruvian food for us at Teresa's apartment, and after we had waited for *hours*, he treated us with the most amazing meal, including homemade *ceviche.*[40] I had never tried ceviche before, and I immediately fell in love with it. After the impactful experience of the summer I had spent in Peru at age eighteen, I was intrigued and excited to have made a Peruvian friend in Japan who was eager to share his culture with us.

Carlos also had no lack of advice about any topic—but he didn't come across as a know-it-all. Rather, he always tried to be helpful. During my second summer in Japan, I was heading home to Canada for the first time for a one-week vacation, and he offered one pertinent suggestion.

My trip home was scheduled for June, the beginning of what was sure to be a hot summer. Summer temperatures often rise to the low- to mid-30s in Fujisawa, and with the humidity, I found the weather stifling. I much preferred the other seasons in Japan even though at home, summer is my favourite. I'm just not a fan of humidity.

Earthquakes can occur at any time of year, at any severity, and without warning. Because of this, Carlos suggested that before I leave for Canada, I empty and then unplug the fridge and unplug any other electrical appliances. This would reduce the chance of an electrical fire should there be an earthquake while I was gone. This sounded logical,

---

[40] Ceviche: a fresh, tasty dish made from raw fish that is cured or quickly pickled in salt and lime juice. Ingredients vary but typically include onion, chili peppers, and tomatoes. Various types of fish can be used. Carlos's version contained octopus.

so I diligently ate up everything in my fridge and unplugged it before I left for Narita to fly home.

My trip home was a whirlwind. I had five days off work plus the weekends enveloping those days, so with flight time factored in, I really only had six days at home. Still, I felt that since more than a year had gone by, going back to Alberta at this point was a good chance to visit people that I missed and reconnect with home. Being home gave my brain a rest from the steady onslaught of new cultures and languages that came with living in Japan and travelling throughout Asia. I also wanted to restock on some supplies that I couldn't get in Japan—or that I *could* get, but I still wanted my favourite Canadian brands of items. I returned to Japan rejuvenated, happy to have seen so many of the important people in my Canadian life, and ready to forge ahead for another year and a half in Japan, maybe longer.

On the train back to Fujisawa after a week of shopping, eating, and visiting in Canada, my monstrous duffle bag and another soft suitcase were stuffed full of clothes I had bought and treats friends and family had given me. (I never bought clothes in Japan because I although I am short, I am not nearly as tiny around the belly as Japanese women are, so I made sure to stock up on another year's supply of clothes. Ironically, because my feet are tiny, I had no trouble finding shoes in Japan. My shoe size is, in fact, average compared to Japanese women although I can get away with buying children's shoes in Canada.)

Japanese people are inconceivably gracious and kind. At Tōkyō Station, where I had to change trains, I struggled with moving my bags from one train platform to the next to catch the train to Fujisawa. A middle-aged businessman saw me clumsily trying to heave my bags up the stairs to get to the platform I needed, and he grabbed my duffle bag. Without a word, he carried it to the top of the stairs. This could very likely happen back home, or in any other country, but he didn't stop there. He went all the way to Fujisawa with me to help me get my bags off the train at the Fujisawa station, and that is where he left me. No ulterior motive, no hitting on me, no expectation for any kind of reward—financial or otherwise. As he left me, I bowed deeply (the deeper the bow, the greater respect it shows) and said an emphatic *dōmo arigatō gozaimasu*!![41] I knew he had gone out of his way because when we disembarked at Fujisawa station, he headed toward the platform to get on a train taking him back the way we had come.

People like this man served as excellent examples for me and a reminder that whenever I travel—or whenever travellers come to my country—I, too, am a representative of my culture and my country. The experience a non-Canadian has with me may forever implant a certain image in their brain, and if I am the only Canadian someone encounters throughout their life, they may view all of Canada through what I have presented through my actions. I learned to try and mindfully be a positive representative of my country and culture regardless of my location or circumstances.

The Japanese people taught me how easy and impactful it is to be a decent, kind, gracious representative of your country and culture. I never saw that man again, and I never knew his name. I barely spoke to him other than to profusely thank him for being so helpful. But that experience continues to serve as a reminder that it is can be just as easy for strangers to be kind and helpful to one another as it is to be rude and disrespectful. Sometimes, being kind, helpful, and generous can be

---

[41] Dōmo arigatō gozaimasu: thank you very much—the most formal expression of thanks in the Japanese language. Dōmo can be used for a quick, informal thanks.

more difficult if it means going out of your way as this man did for me, but isn't it worth making the effort if the effort helps someone in need?

Getting the rest of the way back to my apartment wasn't so bad because I only had one train stop from Fujisawa and then a few minutes' walk from the train station to my apartment. And honestly, if I had left one of my suitcases at the train station and opted to take one bag at a time to my apartment, Japan was a perfectly safe country in which to do so. My bag would have been waiting for me at the station ten minutes later. (That same summer, Mark had been in a park playing soccer with some friends one Sunday afternoon, and the next day, he realized he had left his video camera on a bench in the park. Naturally, he didn't expect to ever see the camera again, but he went back to the park and there it was—on the park bench exactly where he had left it almost twenty-four hours previously.)

By the time I got home, it was late and I was exhausted after the long day of travelling and fighting with my bags. I decided to go straight to bed and worry about unpacking and getting groceries after a good night's rest.

The following day, I set out to restock my fridge. But first I plugged it in. As I neared the fridge and moved to grab the cord, an awful smell hit me. I looked around and couldn't see anything near the fridge that could be producing the smell. Odd. I knew I had emptied my fridge before I left. I opened up the fridge, and indeed, it was empty, but the smell was an awful lot stronger. And then I was hit not only by the smell but with the recollection that I hadn't emptied the freezer compartment.

Ooooh ... noooo ...

What not-so-fresh hell was waiting for me in the freezer compartment? I then remembered that I had had a package of chicken in the freezer. Yikes.

I reached toward the door of the freezer compartment expecting to find a package of mouldy, fuzzy, green or black chicken. Instead, when I opened the freezer door, liquid came gushing out, splashing my feet and the floor. Gagging, I glimpsed inside the freezer to see the tray and the plastic that the chicken had been wrapped in, but no sign of any chicken.

As I continued gagging from the putrid odour that now soaked into my socks, I realized the chicken had liquified. There was no solid evidence of chicken meat anywhere. In the heat and humidity of a Japanese summer, even though my fridge and freezer had been closed, the chicken had emulsified, turning into a greasy, liquid stink-bomb that exploded when I opened the freezer door.

Grocery shopping would have to wait until I cleaned up the vile mess and then aired out my fridge and freezer for a while. And I had to change my socks.

CHAPTER 7

STILL STUMBLING IN YEARS ONE AND TWO

Day of the Dead

Obon is a short period in the middle of August when the Japanese honour their dead ancestors. The belief is that ancestors' spirits come back this time of year to visit their living relatives. In North America, we would call it Day of the Dead, but it is usually commemorated in Japan over three to five days, not one. People visit gravesites bringing offerings of food or flowers, perhaps both. Special dances are performed. At the end of Obon, people release floating lanterns on lakes, rivers, or other bodies of water to guide their ancestors' spirits back to the afterworld for another year.

My co-worker Michelle No. 2 arrived in Japan in the middle of August to begin her contract, so the one-year anniversary of her arrival in Japan landed on the first day of Obon the following year. That day, as always, Ken was the first of us to arrive at school. He liked to be alone there to start his day, reading the *Japan Times* (Japan's national English newspaper) and getting his lessons ready for the day.

Ken was also a pretty thoughtful guy. On the morning of Michelle's anniversary, he thought it would be a nice gesture to give her some flowers to commemorate the occasion, so he bought some at the train station on his way to work. He placed them in her classroom on the table where she always sat when she was teaching.

One by one, the rest of us filed in to work that morning. Michelle was usually one of the last to arrive, and this day was no different. I had no idea Ken had bought these flowers. I was sitting in my classroom across the hallway from her room getting my lessons ready for the day when I suddenly heard ear-splitting shrieking coming from Michelle's room.

Well, turns out, poor Ken had bought this "nice, unique" bouquet for Michelle not knowing that this type of flower arrangement was specifically designated for honouring the dead and was only sold during Obon. That's why it caught his eye: He had not, up to that point, seen a bunch of flowers with this colour scheme before. He thought they were pretty and unique. After Ken had put them in her classroom and retreated to his, our Japanese co-worker Yasuko went into Michelle's classroom to drop something off. She saw the "let's honour the dead" flowers sitting where Michelle always sat, and (naturally) immediately assumed that disaster had struck and Michelle was dead. In Yasuko's mind, why else would these specific flowers be in Michelle's spot honouring her?

I knew that Michelle was fine, and it was all I could do not to burst out laughing at Ken's faux pas. The first order of business, however, was to calm down our poor hysterical co-worker, assure her that Michelle was indeed alive and well, and sort out the confusion and misunderstanding. Once everyone figured out what exactly had happened, we all had a good laugh just as Michelle walked in. Oblivious to all that had just happened—and to the meaning of these types of flowers—Michelle immediately saw the flowers, gushed on about how lovely they were, and thanked Ken profusely. Meanwhile, poor Yasuko went into her classroom to get some colour back into her face and slow her heart rate.

Project Run Away

During my second summer in Japan, I received a greeting card and letter in the mail from a friend back home who had just broken up with her boyfriend. The front of the card had a cartoon of a woman sitting at a desk with the caption, "There comes a point in life when a woman asks herself ..." and the inside of the card finished with, "... do I really deserve the kind of men I attract?"

The sentiment on that card pretty much sums up that part of my life, as well, and that's another book entirely, except for this next section.

Around the time I received that card, I also got a letter from my sister requesting a picture of Mount Fuji. If I went to the closest beach to my apartment, I could see the volcano in the distance, but I had found that it was difficult to get a good picture of it because the sky was often hazy.

One summer Sunday morning, I was, again, catching the 5:08 a.m. train home after spending the night hanging out with my friends playing pool because I had missed the last train. Through the window of the train, I saw one of the clearest views of Mount Fuji I had seen up to that point. There wasn't a cloud in the bright morning sky, and the beautiful cap of snow on the iconic mountain proudly stood out in the distance. I decided since I didn't have to be anywhere other than home to get some sleep, this was the perfect opportunity to finally grab some pictures. I got off the train at my station, trotted home to grab my camera, and got back to the station in time to catch the next train and head down to the beach.

Few people were out and about yet, so the atmosphere at the beach that morning was fresh, clean, and quiet. The only signs of life were local fishermen and their flopping catches.

I found a prime location for photo snapping, and snap away I did.

Within moments, I made a new friend. While I continued taking pictures, a middle-aged Japanese man approached me and, as I surmised by his body language and my weak Japanese, offered to take some pictures of me with Mount Fuji in the background. Mighty nice of him, so I accepted his offer. After all, when would I ever again get the chance to pose for such a photo?! He was perfectly polite, took several photos, but then decided we were now best friends. He put his arm around my shoulder and started babbling away in Japanese. From what I could understand, I surmised that he wanted to have breakfast with me.

Now, every country, every culture, has its fair share of men who hit on foreign women. In Japan, I was a lot more comfortable with this scenario than I have been in some other cultures where the men are more aggressive and unnerving. Even the "creepy old men" in Japan are just ... really polite.

As this man was blathering away, we started walking toward the train station together. I wasn't rude, and I knew I wasn't in any danger, but I was madly planning my exit from this situation as we walked. He kept babbling even though I assumed he knew I couldn't completely understand him. He didn't seem to care. I responded now and then with the odd "Mmmm" (in Japanese, uttering "mmm" is the equivalent of saying "mmm-hmmm" or "uh huh") and the occasional one- or two-word comment. At other times, my instincts and minimal knowledge of the language told me I might be getting myself into something I preferred not to be in so I remained silent.

While he led me toward the train station, I began looking at my watch, looking at the train, making faces, and shaking my head. He politely got the message, accepted my refusal, and then began to interrogate me about my destination. At that point, I feigned complete illiteracy, smiled, and walked away.

He had taken great pictures, at least.

Giant Babies

For someone who has hated getting up early my entire life (so much so I was born five days past my due date), I spent a lot of time on "first trains" when I was living in Japan. Admittedly, a lot of those train rides were end-of-the-day trips back home after being out all night, but I also got up early on quite a few occasions to take long day trips. One of my goals in Japan was to soak in as much culture as I possibly could. What better way than to attend a sumo *basho*![42]

Ever been to a professional sporting event? If so, chances are, you have found it is pretty hard, if not impossible, to get prime seats. The same goes for sumo. All the best seats are permanently bought up by companies and dignitaries. Attending a sumo basho is as big of a deal in Japan as it is to take a client to see an NBA, NFL, or NHL game

[42] Basho: tournament

in corporate Canada or the US. And, of course, front row center is the goal. For myself, my students who wanted to take me to see sumo, and any other plebians who didn't have the prime seats locked up for generations, seating was limited, to say the least. The only seats available were not only in the nosebleed section but *only* in the top row of seats. To even attempt to get tickets, the only option at that time was to get in line at the venue's ticket booth as early as possible in hopes of getting day-of seats for those spots in the rafters. Ah, life before the Internet.

A sumo basho takes place over the course of two weeks. Each day, competitions start in the morning and continue through the evening. Upon acquiring tickets, we entered as soon as we could to claim our seats. The tickets we received admitted us for the entire day, and even though our seats were sky high, we could see quite well, and the atmosphere was unique and exciting.[43] We spent the next several hours alternating between watching the show, getting something to eat, and snoozing. The matches throughout the day take place between less skilled, less famous wrestlers; the superstars come out later in the afternoon and evening. A sumo basho is like a concert festival in that way: the later in the day, the bigger the stars. Therefore, there are hours of matches during the day that most people don't even care to watch. I wasn't too concerned about who we were watching since I had no idea

---

[43] In the summer of 2021, while working on this book, I was again filled with natsukashii while watching the Tōkyō Olympics. The wrestling and boxing matches took place in the *Kokugikan*, Tōkyō's sumo stadium. The sailing competitions were held at the Enoshima Yacht Club, which didn't exist when I lived in Japan. Still, when I saw the aerial views of Enoshima, the small island that was a short boardwalk trek off the beach I spent so much time on during my summers in Fujisawa, my eyes teared up. I was last in Japan in 2001, and I so desperately want to go back again soon!

who the superstars were and didn't care. I just wanted to take in Japan's unique national sport.

My attitude quickly changed. During the day, a lot of the better seats sat empty since the headliners weren't on until later, but as the afternoon wore on, the seats below us began to fill up. The buzz of the crowd slowly got louder and buzzier, and the excitement built slowly and steadily. And then the vibe jettisoned. The big guns were up, and it was like being at a playoff game in any of the sports leagues at home. The atmosphere became an exciting ruckus.

Sumo is odd. Spectators pay big bucks and wait with great anticipation to see superstar wrestlers, who, in Japan, are of the status of someone like Wayne Gretzky or Michael Jordan. These wrestlers train for years for a match that could be over in two seconds. Each match is typically quick, and the basic rules of sumo are simple. A wrestler wins for one of two reasons. Either they cause their opponent to touch the ground with any part of their body other than their feet, or they push their opponent out of the ring (one foot counts as out). Different techniques, moves, and holds are allowed (or not), but the goal is straightforward: knock your opponent off balance. That's really it. Some matches could last several minutes, but it's not uncommon for a match to start and end while you are looking down to grab a handful of popcorn from your bag. Despite the rapid-fire turnover of matches, the sport is exciting, loud, and fascinating. It was definitely worth getting up early for.

Everyone knows that sumo wrestlers are huge, even by western standards. Wrestlers must be a minimum of five feet, seven inches tall, but many tower well over six feet. The minimum weight is 165 pounds, but the stereotypical image of a sumo wrestler is a rotund man. Indeed, many of them are well over 300 pounds, much of which is actually muscle.

And then there is the *mawashi*—the loincloth wrestlers wear when training and competing—which we in North America often crudely and rudely compare to a diaper. The mawashi serves two main purposes. First, of course, it covers up certain body parts and keeps everything in place. The mawashi is also the main tool competitors use to try to throw their rivals off balance since there is nothing else to grab onto except hair and skin—and hair pulling is not allowed. (Wrestlers who pull on their opponents' topknots immediately lose the match). Grabbling the other wrestler by the mawashi and attempting to throw them is a common move in sumo. It's astounding to see how strong these men are when they are successful with this move, completely picking up their massive opponent by the waistband.

Festivals

Japan has a plethora of other traditional events and festivals worth attending. One of my favourites was the annual display of *yabusame*[44] in Kamakura, a small city next to Fujisawa along the coast. Yabusame represents the spirit of samurai history and culture. Every year in late April, archery targets are set up along the dirt road leading toward the Hachimangū Shrine, the largest and most important Shinto shrine in Kamakura. During the day, archers on horseback dressed in samurai costumes compete in a display of archery, running their horses at full speed down the dirt road and shooting at the targets. It's an exciting spectacle to see in person and an impressive throwback to ancient times.

---

[44] Yabusame: archery on horseback

Summer in Japan is festival madness. The Japanese love their fireworks (or *hanabi*[45])—and for good reason; fireworks in Japan are extravagant. As my first summer in Japan approached, I'd been hearing for weeks from my students and Japanese colleagues how great the fireworks were in Japan, and I was looking forward to seeing them in Kamakura. I planned to leave home about an hour before the fireworks started with my co-worker Michelle, who lived in my apartment building, to *give ourselves lots of time*. Ha. Hilarious.

The train between Fujisawa and Kamakura was crowded, but then it usually was because Kamakura is a huge tourist destination any day of the year for both Japanese and international visitors. When we arrived in Kamakura, we got off the train and were immediately immersed in a sea of people, most of whom were wearing yukata.

Japanese people don't often dress in traditional attire. Both men and women wear two- or three-piece business suits for work (women wear skirts with vests and sometimes jackets), and schoolchildren wear uniforms for school. Semi-formal western attire is normal outside of the workplace. But on special occasions, such as weddings or festivals, Japanese people seem to be excited for a reason to wear kimono and yukata. Yukata are most appropriate for the summer festivals since they are lighter. They are made of cotton and are therefore cooler and less formal than kimono. Up to this point, I had seen people wearing yukata on the street from time to time in the summer. And it was particularly easy to spot a sumo wrestler out in public because of their size, ubiquitous topknot, and yukata. But many people don yukata when attending festivals. Anytime I attended one, I felt like I had been transported in time or onto a movie set simply

---

[45] Hanabi: fireworks. In Japanese, hana means flower and bi means fire, so the word literally means fire flower—an appropriately poetic way to describe fireworks.

because of the "dress code." The attire was starkly different from the average daily scene in Japan with crowds of people wearing western clothing, mostly in navy or dark brown.

Michelle and I headed toward the beach to try and find a good spot to view the fireworks. The sun was setting. Shortly after exiting the train station, however, we encountered a problem. The crowd stopped moving. Hmm. Everyone around us was at a standstill, and we had only gotten half a block from the train station. Ah, the crowd started moving again, but after we took six or seven steps, it stopped yet again. People were pushing me from behind. Step. Step. Pause. Step. Pause. Push. I was getting hot. (Summer evenings in Japan don't cool down like they do in Alberta.) Step. Push. Step.

Pop. Pop. Pop. What was that noise? It sounded like a gun. *Pop. Pop pop poppoppoppop*. Oh. The fireworks must have started. *Pop poppoppoppop.* We were now a block away from the train station. *Pop poppoppoppop.* Hmm. We still hadn't made much progress. Step. *Pop poppoppoppop.* You'd think we could see the fireworks in the sky from where we were, but no. *Pop poppoppoppop*. Step. Step. *Pop poppoppoppop.*

It was 7:15 p.m. *poppoppoppop* and we weren't *poppoppoppop* seeming to be making much *poppoppoppop* progress. Step. *Poppoppoppop.* Were we ever *poppoppoppop* going to *poppoppoppop* get to a *poppoppoppop* place where *poppoppoppop* we could see any *poppoppoppop* of the fireworks? *Poppoppoppop.* We weren't *poppoppoppop* moving any more *poppoppoppop*. We *poppoppoppop* hadn't *poppoppoppop* moved *poppoppoppop* for *poppoppoppop* a *poppoppoppop* few *poppoppoppop* minutes *poppoppoppop*. People *poppoppoppop* were *poppoppoppop* elbowing *poppoppoppop* me *poppoppoppop* and *poppoppoppop* then *poppoppoppop* we *poppoppoppop* suddenly *poppoppoppop* gained *poppoppoppop* a *poppoppoppop* few *poppoppoppop* more *poppoppoppop* steps.

Oh! *Poppoppoppop* Suddenly, I *poppoppoppop* could *poppoppoppop* see *poppoppoppop* the *poppoppoppop* fireworks *poppoppoppop* going *poppoppoppop* off *poppoppoppop* over *poppoppoppop* the *poppoppoppop* ocean *poppoppoppop poppoppoppop POPPOPPOPPOP POPPOPPOPPOP POPPOPPOPPOP POPPOPPOPPOP POPPOPPOPPOP.*

Silence.

They were done. We had seen all of a few seconds of them.

And, oh no ... suddenly, the crowd in front of us had turned around and was facing us. Thousands of people were now coming back our way.

We turned around.

Step.

Step.

Step.

I could hear Michelle saying to me, "The train's going to be packed, and we'll be waiting forever for room on a train to get back to Fujisawa. Let's outsmart the crowd and take the bus."

Great idea.

We ducked out of the crowd at the next intersection and snuck around the corner.

Ahhhhhhhhh. Free from the crowd. Room to move. Room to breathe. The next challenge was to find a bus stop.

Within a few minutes, we found a bus stop and checked that it was a stop for buses going to Fujisawa. Yep. And right away, the bus came along. What luck!!

The bus stopped, and we got on. It was packed. Well, by our Canadian standards it was packed, which meant we had to stand. By Japanese standards, there was plenty of room! (The rumours are true. There really are people who work at the train stations whose job is to shove people onto the trains. Particularly during rush hour, it's no exaggeration to say that the trains and buses can be so full—and people are jammed so closely together—that you could lift your feet off the ground and remain in position. For those of us who love our personal space, especially on public transit, this is all a little too cozy.)

The bus left the stop and drove away ... for about fifteen seconds, when we turned a corner. And then the bus stopped. And there we sat. Hmm. A theme to our evening was starting to emerge.

Time passed, and we opened the windows of the bus. We changed position. We shifted from one foot to another. We switched our arms that were holding the handrails. We switched again. There were no more windows to open, but we could barely tell because everyone on the bus was sweating and sweltering. Michelle and I were getting exhausted from standing since we had left home two hours prior and most of all, I was wondering WHOSE BRAINY IDEA WAS IT TO TAKE THE BUS?

The light bulb went on right about then. Trains don't have to stop for traffic jams. Buses do. Why had we not thought before getting on the bus that of course traffic coming from the beach back to the city was going to be a nightmare? The train, packed as it would have been, wouldn't have been MUCH more packed than the bus, AND AT LEAST IT WOULD HAVE BEEN MOVING. Argh.

I kept all of these screaming thoughts inside my head, though, and after losing about ten pounds through sweating on that hellish bus for about an hour, we got off somewhere in Kamakura and started hoofing it to the nearest train station, Gokurakuji, which was about a third of the way back to Fujisawa.

We boarded the next train, which was ... SURPRISE, packed, and stood on that creaky thing for the twenty-minute ride back to Fujisawa.

When all was said and done, the half-hour trip to Fujisawa took us two hours. Wiping what sweat was still oozing out of my body on the stairs up to my apartment, I thought, yes, fireworks festivals in Japan are something to experience.

Mr. Poop

Everything in Japan is cute. *"Kawaii!!"* meaning cute or adorable, is an exclamation that regularly comes out of the mouths of girls throughout the country, especially Japanese high school girls and college-age women. Even middle-aged housewives can be seen toting Hello Kitty purses or Pikachu bentō boxes. Since my stint in Japan, Canada and the rest of the world have experienced an invasion of these Japanese characters in our movie theatres, clothing stores, and technology.

One day, Tomoko and I were shopping in a small Shop Full of Cute Things. Among the stationery, little coin purses, charms, and children's bentō boxes, many of which were pink or yellow, I saw some brown items in the shape of a puffy triangle ... with eyes. I paused, tilted my head, and cautiously looked around to see if anyone was watching me.

Is that ...? I thought to myself as I gingerly picked up one of these little coin purses. I couldn't believe that's what it would be, but I couldn't think of what else this little character was supposed to represent. After all, I was in The Land of Unrelenting Politeness. There was no way such a polite culture would sell coin purses in the shape of a turd … with eyes.

Tomoko saw me holding the mysterious brown coin purse and came over to me.

I gave her a quizzical look and asked her, "Is this what I think it is?"

She started to giggle and told me, "That's Unchi-kun!"

I then looked around and noticed that various "Unchi-kun" items were dispersed throughout the shop. Obviously, this Unchi-kun, whoever he was, was kind of a big deal.

I replied, "Well, I know that '-kun' means sort of like 'mister' for boys, but I don't know what 'unchi' means."

By this time, I was comfortable enough with Tomoko to talk about pretty much anything. I leaned a bit closer and whispered to her, "It looks like a piece of poo!"

And she laughed a little more loudly.

"Yes!" She confirmed. "'Unchi' means poop!" she explained. "Not 'shit.' 'Poop.'"

"So this is an actual character in Japan? Like Hello Kitty?" I asked. "And his name is Mr. Poop?"

She assured me that was the case, and that he was indeed terribly … "poopular." (My word, not hers. Har Har.)

Well, I thought Unchi-kun was the most hilarious thing I had heard of in a while, and I bought a squishy little Unchi-kun stress ball for myself.

Fast forward roughly twenty years … Imagine my surprise when Unchi-kun immigrated to Canada (and beyond) making his appearance in the emoji selections on my cellphone and in the prize selection of stuffies at the Calgary Stampede midway! Now, every time someone sends Unchi-kun to me on my social media or text messages, I can't help but think back and smile at my bemusement when I first learned about Japan's endearing little piece of feces … with eyes. A national treasure.

Take Me Anywhere

Roughly a year after I had arrived, one of the members of my social group got a new co-worker from Seattle. Stephen had been in Japan for a year already but transferred from another school to one in our area. He was goofy and easy to get along with. He slipped easily into the friendship I had built with Mark by this time, and the three of us had our own little side friendships in addition to the whole group dynamic. Sometimes I would hang out with Mark, sometimes Stephen and I did things together, and sometimes the two of them hung out. Often the three of us got together. In November of my second year (1993), the two November national holidays close to one other meant that if we took one vacation day off of work, we would have a five-day "weekend." That September, Mark, Stephen, and I decided to travel together somewhere during the November holiday.

We talked about a potential vacation a couple of times and quickly decided to book ourselves some flights somewhere that month. The problem was that we made this decision the day before I was leaving to travel elsewhere in Japan for a long weekend in September. Mark and Stephen weren't going anywhere that weekend, so I left them instructions to go ahead and book the trip while I was gone if they found a good deal.

We had agreed upon a budget—a maximum of US$500 per person for flights—and that was our only criteria. For that price, we could easily get anywhere in Asia, and being as it was a five-day trip, we didn't want to go somewhere terribly far anyway and spend half the time in transit. At this point, the only travelling I had done outside of Japan was to Australia and the three-day getaway to Seoul with Brian and Michelle.

I told Mark and Stephen, "You know what I like to do when I travel, and we all like the same things. As long as it's not Seoul, just pick a place you want to go and book the ticket for me. If you find a good deal, book it while I'm gone and I will pay you when I get back."

When I returned from my long weekend, Mark told me they had bought tickets for the three of us and the price came out right around our $500 maximum. I paid him and thanked him.

He gave me a funny look and asked, "Don't you want to know where we are going?"

I paused, returned the smile, and said, "You know what? Actually, I don't. Just tell me what kind of clothes to pack—whether I need beach clothes or hiking clothes or winter clothes—and I'll follow you to the airport. I trust you."

And so the great mystery trip was booked. For the next several weeks, friends and co-workers kept poking at me, confirming that I really didn't want to know. After the first couple of weeks, everyone knew where I was going except me. I just shrugged my shoulders and said, "Nah, I trust them." I did walk into my classroom one day and caught Ken and Mark looking at the world map on my wall, but Mark had just finished pointing out to Ken on the map where we were going.

So even though they had looked guilty when they saw me walk into the room, I was no wiser. We were going somewhere in the world; I knew that much.

Unfortunately, a while later, one of my friends who didn't know I was within earshot mentioned "when Lorna goes to Thailand with Mark and Stephen"—so that part of the cat's body was sticking plainly out of the bag.

In late November, Mark, Stephen, and I headed to the airport, beach clothes in tow, for our short trip to Thailand. Narita is a handy airport. There are direct flights to a lot of places in the world from Tōkyō, and flights to other Asian countries are short because each is a mere hop over a lot of ocean. In this case, the water we flew over was in the South China Sea and the Gulf of Thailand during a five-hour flight to Bangkok.

But no, Bangkok was not our final destination. We boarded another smaller plane for a short hop down to Phuket. Ah, now it made sense. Phuket. Thus the beach clothes. I had heard of Phuket as a great beach destination and was excited they had chosen this as our destination.

Nope—still not our final location. I was instructed to follow them as we set out on foot in Phuket to the shore, where they looked for a boat. Hmm—where exactly were we going? Shouldn't we be finding a place to stay before we go fishing or something? Yep, we would, but not here. Stephen and Mark nabbed a guy with a boat, we boarded, and Boat Dude launched his motor into high gear, sending us blasting through the crystal blue waters. I looked at Mark and Stephen; they looked at me and laughed. Finally, I asked, "So where ARE we actually going?"

Ko Phi Phi (pronounced Ko Pee Pee) is a tiny island off the mainland with white sand beaches and a small village. When we arrived, we disembarked, paid our "taxi" driver, and finally set out to find a place to stay. The guys hadn't booked accommodations in advance because everything we had ever read about Thailand recommended to just go, find a little cabin on the beach, and negotiate the rate on the spot.

Because there were three of us, we needed a slightly larger cabin than most backpackers who came through the area at that time. We ended up finding a great little two-room cabin (one room being the bathroom) that was steps from the beach with two double beds. We got our tiny cabin for US$30 a night, which was about three times what we had thought we would pay, but we did need the extra bed. The rate was still a steal compared to Japanese and Canadian prices, especially since the room also included the delightful geckos that hung stuck on the walls the whole time we were there. They *were* alive; even though I never saw them move, they were in different spots on the wall anytime we came back from the beach or a restaurant.

It was a perfect little getaway. The beds in our cabin were comfy. They didn't come with blankets—not that we needed any though in the tropical heat—and everything we needed was a few minutes' walk away: the beach, restaurants, shops. Other than temporarily being mystified as to how to flush the toilet—turns out we were to fill the bucket that was provided in the bathroom with water and pour it down the toilet—all was perfect. That is, except for Mark getting sick. Which happened almost immediately after our arrival.

After a full day of travelling, we were naturally hungry, so we wandered around until we found some food options that looked good. And they *were* good. But for some reason, whatever Mark ate or drank didn't agree with him, and he was sick the whole weekend shortly after that meal. Stephen and I felt fine the entire time, so it remained a mystery as to why Mark got hit and the rest of us didn't since we ate from the same restaurant. Whatever Mark caught was some sort of stomach bug that gave him the chills and a fever.

The three of us didn't do much during the weekend other than hang out at the beach, relaxing and swimming. Although we all stuck together the whole weekend, Mark never did go in the water. Instead, he sat on the beach, wrapped in his beach towel, shivering with the chills while Stephen and I enjoyed the warm water. We felt bad for him, but he wasn't so sick that he needed medical care (or maybe he did but we just didn't think to take him back to the mainland. Nice friends you have, Mark!). At any rate, there wasn't anything we could do for him. He … *sort of* enjoyed the trip … at least as best he could. Mark is a positive and laid-back guy, so there was no complaining from him even though I'm sure he was miserable.

Three Days, Three Ways

After my first Christmas abroad in Australia, I decided to spend the second in Japan, working. (Yes, here is where you are to feel sorry for me, although working on Christmas Day was my choice.)

Christmas Day isn't a national holiday in Japan, so rather than taking any days off, I worked on December 25 prior to going away over the New Year national holidays. I tried to convince myself that Christmas would be just like any other day (since in Japan it pretty much was), but the sentiment of the day did get to me. I couldn't help thinking that back home, once again, my family was gathering for turkey and spending time with each other eating all of the other treats we only got at Christmastime. It was a tough day. Getting *mikan*[46] in Japan more easily and for a longer period of time than in Canada—and the fact that they tasted so much fresher and better than the ones we got at home at Christmastime—was little consolation.

I embraced my woefulness and showed Dr. Seuss's *The Grinch Who Stole Christmas* cartoon to all of my classes that day, using it to generate a "cultural lesson" and discussion on what Christmas means to us in Canada. I still feel a bit guilty about copping out that day because, let's face it, Dr. Seuss isn't the greatest choice of learning materials for teaching the English language. But my gracious students, I think, understood how difficult it was for me to be away from home and working on the most significant holiday in my culture. They humoured me by at least feigning interest in the surly green creature. My favourite response to the video was from Naoto, one of my more advanced students: "His body looks like an eggplant."

The main thought keeping my chin up on Christmas Day was knowing that Ken and I had booked flights to Singapore, where we were going over the Japanese national holidays, New Year's Day, and the following few days. Neither of us took any extra days off that holiday season, instead planning our travels around the five days we had off for the holidays. Days one and five were for travel, which left us three days in Singapore. Since the country is small, we figured three days was plenty of time to see everything there was to see.

Turns out one day was enough for us. Singapore is a *beautiful* city and country, and the Christmas lights and decorations all over were elegant and stunning. Upon arrival, we quickly found accommodation

---

[46] Mikan: The little "mandarin" oranges that I have always called "Christmas oranges" because that's the only time of year we get them in Canada. They are plentiful in Japan in the winter and much tastier than the ones we get in Canada.

in Little India, one of the many cultural districts, and got up early on the first day to explore. We checked everything off our list that we wanted to see and do on that first full day: enjoying the Singapore Botanic Gardens, exploring Chinatown, and of course getting a token tourist photo with the Merlion statue. We mainly walked and explored, appreciating the Christmas decorations and making mental notes of how and where the city's cultural divides—such as Little India, Chinatown, and the colonial district—were situated.

We ended our day with dinner at a restaurant, where we discussed what we would do on our second and third days. We decided that the proximity to Malaysia and Indonesia allowed us the opportunity to get a few more stamps in our passports before heading back to Japan. Three days, three countries? We could do it!

Singapore has, for decades, been known as one of the cleanest cities in the world. We knew before heading there that chewing gum was banned, so I had double-checked my purse and suitcase to make sure I wasn't bringing contraband into the country. Singapore imposes hefty fines on people who litter and even on those who don't flush the toilet. I was a little bit on edge the whole day because I knew the "garbage police" in Singapore were more diligent than they were in Japan and I didn't want to end up in garbage jail.[47]

After eating, I needed to use the bathroom before we headed back to our beds for the night. To my horror, after I was finished depositing my contribution to Singapore's sewage system, I discovered that the toilet didn't flush. It was broken. I jiggled and wiggled any parts I could find that might prompt the toilet to come to life.

Nothing.

---

[47] There wasn't an official "garbage police force," but the rules in Singapore were strict and punishments for littering, etc., were harsh.

I finally resigned myself to the fact that I was about to become a criminal in an Asian country. One with merciless punishments for law-breaking.

Having gained slightly more intelligence over the years, I now recognize that the appropriate course of action would have been to approach one of the staff members, ask them to accompany me to the bathroom, and show them that the toilet was not working so that they would know I had honestly tried to be a good visitor. However, although I had lived abroad for almost two years at that point, I was still fairly naive and shy in culturally different situations. Even to this day, when I'm in an unfamiliar situation and not 100 per cent confident about what I should or should not be doing, I often default to my naturally shy nature, doing nothing for fear of looking like a doofus. I tentatively stepped out of the bathroom, looking around to see if anyone was watching me, and quickly trotted back to our table.

"We need to get out of here. Now!!" I loudly whispered to Ken, as if I had just robbed a bank, hurriedly grabbing my purse.

"What …" he started.

"I'll tell you outside," I scream-whispered at him. "LET'S JUST GO. NOW!"

We quickly paid for our meal and left the restaurant. As we walked away, I told him how and why we were now officially fugitives from the potty police.

And so we fled the country the next day, hopping a bus and heading north into Johor Bahru, the first city on the Malaysian side of the border. From downtown Singapore to Johor Bahru was approximately a one-hour bus ride. We visited Istana Besar, the royal palace and pretty much the only tourist attraction in the area. We didn't really care what we saw or did; our goal was to be able to say we had visited three countries in three days while sleeping in the same country for the whole trip. So in Johor Bahru, we explored and found a place to have lunch.

Singapore is a culturally rich and diverse city and country. With its proximity to Malaysia and the rest of Asia, Singapore consists of a great mix of Indian, Malay, Thai, Chinese, Taiwanese, and Filipino people. We were eager to soak up a taste of as many of these cultures as we could, so for lunch in Johor Bahru, we scoped out a tiny local restaurant, knowing it would certainly be offering up traditional Malaysian food. Sure enough, we ordered a sampling of rice, meat, and vegetables all served on a large banana leaf. But no cutlery.

We had known ahead of time that Malaysians eat with their hands, and this was exactly why we wanted to find a hole-in-the-wall local restaurant: we wanted an authentic experience. I also knew ahead of time that Malaysian people eat food with their right hands only. The left hand is considered unclean, and I had been told that one of the reasons is that people wipe themselves with their left hand after going to the bathroom. Well, I am left-handed.

I gave it the old college try and started trying to scoop the rice and meat with my right hand. It was a complete disaster. Ken, who was right-handed, wasn't doing a whole lot better, but he was managing to get some food into his mouth while I was just dropping everything. Of course, we were giggling at ourselves for being inept at feeding ourselves. After a few more fruitless attempts with my right hand, I looked at Ken, shook my head, and said, "Screw it. I'm going to starve if I keep this up," and switched to my left hand. I fared a bit better, managing to get about half of what I attempted to scoop up to stay in my hand and make it to my mouth with each shoveling motion.

We were making a huge mess of our banana leaf "plates," our faces, our clothes, the table, and the floor, and of course we were laughing harder and harder the messier we got. Two local men were in the restaurant sitting off to the side, slightly behind Ken. They could see us and I could see them. They started giggling and staring at us a bit. Then, as our laughter and messiness grew, so did their laughter. By the end of the meal, there was rice all over our table, our shirts, our hands, and our arms, and they were laughing heartily along with me and Ken. I don't know if their laughter was inspired by us laughing at ourselves or if they were laughing at these two foreigners trying largely unsuccessfully to feed themselves. I was also wondering if they were possibly laughing at the fact that I was eating with my bum-wiping hand. Probably all three. In the end, they were laughing at us and with us, the meal was delicious, and we were sufficiently both fed and entertained by our antics and their laughter. We gave them a huge smile as we left the restaurant.

On our third full day, Ken and I headed in the opposite direction for another stamp in our passports. Batam Island is a tiny Indonesian island accessible to the south of Singapore by a one-hour ferry ride. We took the trip across the water and spent the day roaming the markets, trying local food, and buying a few souvenirs. Again, we didn't have any burning desire to do anything specific other than explore a little and get that stamp on our passports. Check.

We boarded our plane to Japan the next day proud that we had knocked three countries off our travel list—and carrying the proof in our passports. I have kept every passport that has ever been issued to me since I started travelling in my teens. The one that was valid during my time in Asia is by far the one with the most stamps. Every once in a while, I open it up to see the colourful visitor visa for Australia, the multiple entry stamps for Japan, and the proof that Ken and I, while sleeping four nights in Little India, Singapore and using it as our anchor point, visited three countries in three days.

CHAPTER 8

TREATS FROM HOME

I lived in Japan before the days of the Internet. My school didn't even have a computer the whole time I was there, which I thought was odd. By the early '90s, people were starting to buy personal computers, and with Japan being so technologically ahead of Canada in most regards, one would think it would have been the first adopters of sleek new computers. Everything in my school though was done over the phone, on paper, by fax, and by snail mail.

Several months before I moved back to Canada, I received a letter from a friend who asked me if I had an email address and if I did, could I pass it on to her so she could write to me more quickly and easily. I had no idea what she was talking about, so when I answered her letter, I simply didn't address her question.

In Japan, I made a point of phoning my mom once a week since phone calls were obviously faster than writing letters. I knew she worried about me being so far away, and I also knew my extended family often asked her how and what I was doing, so I made sure I kept in touch. Plus, talking weekly was just what my mom and I did. We talked on the phone, on average, once a week from the time I moved away from home at seventeen until she died years after I had returned from Japan. My phone bills in Japan averaged around C$200 a month, but that was one of the areas in which I was willing to spend the money. I have always been strongly connected to my family, and those phone calls were just as much for my comfort as they were for her reassurance that I was thriving in this vastly different, faraway land.

What Earthquake?

One of the phone calls I got from my mom was quite alarming. It was January 1995. I had submitted my resignation and was preparing to make the move back to Canada. Even after almost three years, my Japanese language skills were still rudimentary because I spent so much of my time using English both at work and in my free time, so even though I had a TV and radio, my main source of news was the daily *Japan Times*, the English newspaper, which arrived at our school every morning.

On the morning of January 17, I arrived at work having no reason to think it wasn't like any other day. I read that day's *Japan Times*, and I was preparing for my first lesson when my manager came blasting through my classroom door telling me my mom was on the phone.

What?!? In nearly three years, my mom had never called me at work. She had the school's phone number in case of emergency, but I knew she would only call the school if there *was* an emergency. I ran to the office, panicking that something horrible had happened to a family member.

"Hello, I'm here. Are you OK?" I immediately queried when I picked up the phone.

"I'm OK," my mom replied. "Are *you* OK?"

"Um, yes, I'm fine," I responded. "You are the one that called me. What's going on?"

"Everybody here is wondering if you are OK," she informed me.

"What?!" I asked her. "Why would you all think I wasn't OK?"

"Well, your grandma and some of your aunts and uncles have been calling me to ask me if you were OK after the earthquake," she explained.

"What earthquake?" I replied.

And so my mom, from the Canadian prairies, explained to me that they were hearing reports of a 6.9 magnitude earthquake hitting the city Kobe—and, of course, causing monumental damage.

"Oh, I haven't heard anything about it," I told her, "and Kobe is three hours from here by train. It's like the distance between Calgary and Edmonton. So no, it hasn't impacted us here at all, and I didn't even know there was an earthquake."

"Well, I thought you would be fine because I knew it was far away, but your family here don't know the geography of Japan, and they were worried that you might have been impacted."

"Nope, I'm fine. You can assure everyone that it was good and far away from here."

I read about the earthquake in the *Japan Times* the next day.

You've Got Mail

My mom was great at sending me packages anytime I needed or missed anything from home. So were lots of friends and other family members. Usually, the packages from home contained treats like licorice, cookies, and deodorant. (For the life of me, I could not find deodorant in Japan, and it took me a while to discover the reason: Japanese people don't use it! For a fascinating explanation as to why, do an Internet search using the words "Asian people," "deodorant," and "earwax.")

One day after work a couple of months after I had arrived, I came home to find an envelope in the mail. As I climbed the stairs to my apartment, I was eager to get inside and tear open the envelope that I was holding with the Canadian stamp and my mom's handwriting on the outside. When I got inside, I ripped open the envelope. Onto the floor fell two pressed prairie crocuses, one of my favourite flowers. I gasped, and tears welled up in my eyes.

As a child growing up on the prairies, I used to roam around our pasture land either on foot or, most often, on horseback. My dog always came along. From as young an age as I can remember, my spring tradition was to pick crocuses for my mom. At the first sighting of crocuses each year, I would seek out the fullest crocus patch I could find, get off my horse, crouch down, and pick a handful of the fuzzy purple flowers. I'd stuff them into my pocket or gently tuck them in-between the saddle and saddle pad. Then I'd bring them back home for my mom, who promptly put them into a cup of water and placed them in the middle of the dining room table. I continued this tradition up to the time I left for Japan. Even when I was a university student, my search for the best crocuses to give to my mom was my first order of business after moving back home at the end of the school year. (They bloom right around the end of April after the university school year has finished.) In 1992, however, for the first time since I was probably four or five, I couldn't pick crocuses for my mom. She had it covered, though.

Fast forward a few more months, and I received another stab in the heart from her. I came home from work to again find an unexpected piece of mail: a small package from my mom. In my last conversation with her, I hadn't mentioned anything specifically or directly to her about how badly the culture shock and homesickness were hitting me at that particular point. Still, she could tell by my tone that I was experiencing a rough patch. She didn't say anything to me about it during the conversation; she responded by sending a package. I was surprised to have received this airmail package because I hadn't asked her to send anything. When I opened it, I was stunned at what I found.

When I was about three years old, my Grandma Stuber made me a rag doll. The doll was made in my likeness: she had brown curly hair and blue eyes, and Grandma clothed her in a soft, pink, flowered dress with matching pink bloomers. That doll never left my bed when I was little, and when I moved away from home to go to university, sentimentality prompted me to bring her along and keep her on my bed. I had come to Japan with a ton of luggage, including my guitar, so I really didn't have room for anything frivolous like a silly doll. In fact, I hadn't even thought to bring her. I was focused on bringing necessities, such as clothes, cold remedies, and other types of medication to tide me over until I figured out what to buy in Japan when I got sick. I had brought the Scruples game and some books to read, not knowing if I'd be able to find English games or books easily.

The box my mom had sent me contained some treats, but on the top was this doll, lying there, staring up at me with her big blue eyes and permanent, painted smile. Her hands were pinned together with a safety pin and projected in front of her body as if she were a diver, ready to swan dive off a diving platform. I opened the pin, pulled out the paper that was pinned between her hands, unfolded it, and read my mom's handwriting:

Dear Lorna,

I heard you were having a hard time and so I came to l live with you. Please don't be sad. You are doing what you dreamed about doing since you were a child and this is the experience of a lifetime. You will have hard times, but keep your chin up. I will be with you for the rest of your time in Japan so that you won't be so lonely when you think about home.

I burst out sobbing uncontrollably. And that silly little doll has been on my bed every place I have lived ever since then.

National Mutilation Department

From the time I was in upper-elementary school and well into high school, I had several pen pals from various countries: Finland, Australia, South Korea, Egypt, Italy, and Germany. Some of these friends were only in my life for a couple of years before we lost touch, but during the time we wrote to each other, some of us also exchanged packages. In my first twenty-one years before moving to Japan, I had sent and received quite a few packages between Canada and other countries as well as domestically. Never had I seen any packages even remotely close to the condition they were in when they arrived at my Japanese apartment from Canada.

For some reason, all of the packages I got from home looked like they had been run over by a train. And I wasn't alone. This phenomenon was an experience shared by every one of the foreign teachers I hung out with. *Every single package* that *every single one of us* received was smashed. It became a running joke. We started referring to Japan Post's special *Mutilation Department*: a fictitious, secret room where packages from Canada and the US addressed to North American teachers living in Japan were diverted so officials could smash them with baseball bats before moving them along to their destinations. Maybe Japanese people, under all of that surface-level politeness, were resentful of us for the licorice and cookies and this was their passive-aggressive way of telling us so? The reason for the condition of our packages remains a mystery.

The Biggest and Best Package

It was written into our contracts that we were to give three months' notice of resignation, so in the autumn of my second year, I notified my school that I intended to extend my contract for another year. Shortly before my two-year contract was up, my mom called me for one of our weekly phone calls. She informed me that she, my aunt Darlene (who had found the job ad in the paper for me), and my sister were planning to come to Japan for two weeks to visit me.

What?! What a treat! I had only seen my family once in two years—the previous June while the chicken was metamorphosizing in my freezer—and I hadn't had any company from home. To have them visit would be so fun. They decided to come a week before Golden Week since I had that time off and could tour them around. My mom had one question for me, though, as they were making their travel plans. She figured that since she had spent a little over a thousand dollars on postage sending me packages for the previous two years, it seemed only fair that she spend the equivalent amount paying for my sister's airfare. Mom wondered what my thoughts were on this. My parents and grandparents always took great care to make sure they treated their kids and grandkids equally. Whatever one got, the others got. I agreed wholeheartedly. That seemed only fair—and besides, if my sister's coming to Japan was dependent on whether Mom paid for her ticket, it was a win for me, too.

As planned, the three of them arrived a week before Golden Week. I met them at Narita and took them back to Fujisawa. I have often wondered what it must have been like for them to witness me guiding them through such a different culture and country, speaking broken Japanese, and helping them maneuver the cultural differences. Buying their train tickets and getting them to Fujisawa was only the beginning of my tour guiding.

They had come on a Friday, and the next day (the end of my workweek), I took them to work with me as guest speakers. My Saturday group lessons were a good mix of students. My afternoon class was my most advanced class, with businessmen and college students. Their English was strong, and most of the class that day was another "cultural lesson." I gave them a chance to ask my family questions about Canada, their lives, and their values while they, in turn, answered my family's questions about Japan. One of my students was even so bold as to ask my mother what she would think if I were to marry a Japanese man and stay in Japan forever. I tried so hard to control my smirk as she diplomatically answered him with what I knew was a difficult response for her to say: "I will support Lorna in whatever she decides to do in life. She makes good decisions, and if she felt that was right for her, I would support her."

Right. I knew darn well Mom would never be OK with me permanently living so far away, but having been in Japan less than twenty-four hours, she was already catching on to how important it is in Japanese society to be polite and diplomatic.

My last class of the week was a group class from 7 to 9 p.m. I had long since dubbed this my Saturday Night Fever class because, in addition to the class being scheduled on a Saturday night, it consisted of a group of businessmen and college students who, despite the age differences, all clicked really well. Along with Michelle's 7 p.m. advanced class, these students often arranged to go out after class to an izakaya or for karaoke together. This group of students' hilarity and energy provided the perfect end to my workweek, and Michelle and I would often join them in going out after class since they were gregarious, funny, and warm.

My family was visiting; this was a special occasion. My students, along with some of Michelle's, were excited to arrange for an official after-school welcome party for my family—at a karaoke studio, of course.

Karaoke in Japan is different from how it is in Canada. At home, I've only been to pubs and bars on karaoke night where the whole bar is subjected to the singing of whoever should happen to grab the mic. (And, in my experience, those singing are almost always people who shouldn't be.)

In Japan, however, karaoke is wildly popular and done with groups of friends, day or night. Karaoke studios are set up in small office-style buildings, and each studio has several rooms. Patrons can rent rooms of various sizes depending on how many are in their group. The rooms are mostly soundproof and usually comfortable. They are equipped with small couches or comfy chairs, a TV screen (two or even three if the room is quite big), and a telephone (used to contact the staff to order food and drinks, which are then brought to the room). Rooms are rented by the hour, and the prices are quite reasonable; it was a fairly cheap and fun form of entertainment and one that I spent a lot of money on. And the bizarre thing is, everyone in Japan is a good singer (or at least the people I always went with were).

My students had planned to take my family and me to a nice karaoke place and treat us to a typical Japanese evening out. The other "most typical evening out" would have been to go to an izakaya, but I think my students wanted to see if my family could sing! Plus, they all knew that I loved karaoke. Hirata-san, one of Michelle's students who was a lovely businessman in his forties, demonstrated the true spirit of being a gracious host. He took it upon himself to order food for all of us and asked everyone, including my family and me, what we would like to drink. We were not asked what we wanted to eat; he wanted to order a good array of Japanese bar foods to give my family the "real" experience.

Drinks arrived and the mic was passed around. Right when the food started coming, it was my turn to sing. Hirata-san sidled up beside my mom and was intent on treating her exceptionally well since she was my mother and a guest in his country. As I was singing, I could see him offering up a bowl of one of the items he had ordered, and I saw her trying it.

When I finished my song, I came back and sat down near them, hearing him praising my mother for raising such a nice daughter with a "velvet voice." This man was charming, polite, kind, and funny. He was someone I had quickly become extremely fond of even though he had never been my student. When I sat down with him and my mom, the discussion turned to the food being passed around. Hirata-san was quite pleased with himself that he was getting my mother to try all kinds of Japanese food she had never seen or heard of before.

Pointing at the bowl I had seen him passing to her while I was singing, I asked my mom, "Did you try that?"

She replied that she had.

"YOU TRIED THAT??" I asked her again, incredulously.

"Yes," she replied again as she gave me a funny look. (Neither my mom nor I would last five minutes in a poker game; I inherited from her the complete inability to hide my feelings by the expressions on my face.)

"Have you ever eaten that?" Mom asked me.

"No way!" I exclaimed as Hirata-san laughed. After two years, I was far past the point of trying everything put in front of me, and he knew it. He also knew he had pulled one over on my mom—and that, had she known what she was eating, she would have likely found a way to politely refuse.

She asked what it was.

"*Shiokara*," was his reply.

I just rolled my eyes and laughed. Of course, my mom had no idea what shiokara was.

I explained to her that she had just sampled a few bites of salted, fermented squid intestines. I could see the battle within her mind to suppress the horror and stop it from coming out through her facial expressions.

"And how was it?" I asked as I smirked at her, already knowing her response from her facial expression.

"It wasn't very good," she said honestly but politely.

Hirata-san laughed heartily. It had been a test, one which she had passed.

More Golden Opportunities to Travel and Learn

The following week, I had to work three days before Golden Week started. I studied my Tōkyō train and subway maps, writing out instructions and directions for my family to get to must-see places in Tōkyō like the Imperial Palace, Tōkyō Tower, a sake distillery, and a few others. Going to Kamakura was easy enough, so they spent a day there, as well. They had no problem getting themselves around during those first few days. I had already taken them into Tōkyō on the weekend to see some sights and attend a *kabuki*[48] performance. This had initiated them to the train system with me as their guide, therefore making them a bit more comfortable than if I had simply pointed them in the right direction and wished them luck.

The only real mishap occurred one morning before we left Fujisawa to travel during Golden Week. My sister had quickly left my apartment and headed to the convenience store on the main floor of my building in search of something to eat for breakfast. There, she bought herself a doughnut, which she quickly spit out when her taste buds informed her that instead of being filled with jam, the doughnut was filled with curry. (She wasn't opposed to curry; it was just not what she was expecting or wanting to eat for breakfast.) When I returned home from work each night, they were already back at my apartment and had enjoyed seeing some of the sights that were good day trips from where I lived.

After three days of my family running amuck without me supervising them (so Lord knows what they really got up to!), Golden Week was upon us. My friend and co-worker, Tomoko, had helped me

[48] Kabuki: Classical Japanese live drama. Kabuki is known for actors' overly dramatic poses, facial expressions, and movements, as well as their extravagant costumes. Kabuki actors are traditionally all male.

pre-buy train tickets for Golden Week, and she was going to be travelling with us. The plan was to take my family to see a good chunk of Japan that I had not yet seen myself. First and foremost, they were excited to be taking the famed shinkansen (the bullet train).

Our first stop was in Ōsaka and Kyōto (two major cities that are only minutes apart), where we stayed for a few days. There's a lot to see and do there, one of the most famous and beautiful attractions being *Kinkaku-ji*,[49] or the Golden Pavilion. Kinkaku-ji is the Zen Buddhist temple in Kyōto that is covered in gold leaf—thus its name.

It was in Ōsaka and Kyōto that I introduced my family to two of my favourite Japanese foods. One is *okonomiyaki*, a pancake-style dish that is much more than batter. While the base is similar to a pancake batter, different meats and vegetables are mixed into it before it is grilled. Every area of Japan has its own style of okonomiyaki, but the base ingredients for all areas are water, flour, and eggs to make the batter, plus shredded cabbage and green onion. Depending on the region—and individual taste—additional mixings and toppings may include pork or bacon, shrimp, octopus, noodles, an egg, and additional vegetables. (When I make it, I like to add bean sprouts.) A special okonomiyaki sauce, similar to a tangy steak sauce, is drizzled on top of the cooked "pancake" along with Japanese mayonnaise. Each okonomiyaki is also usually topped with dried seaweed flakes and dried *bonito*[50] flakes. I've yet to meet anyone from any culture who doesn't love it. Asian supermarkets in Canada sell packaged mixes for the batter as well as the sauce, seaweed, and bonito flakes. Of course, the meat

---

[49] Kin means gold or money, and -ji has a few meanings but one use is as a suffix attached to the name of a temple.

[50] Bonito: a fish, similar to tuna

options, cabbage, and other vegetables can be bought in any grocery store.

The other food I really wanted my family to try was something I knew my mom and aunt would likely *not* try if I told them what it was (though my sister likely would have been game). Without Michelle's and my students around, they would have left the politeness on the train.

Restaurants in Japan specialize in one type of food, such as an okonomiyaki restaurant, so diners wouldn't just go to a restaurant for "Japanese food." Customers need to decide ahead of time what kind of food they want and choose that type of restaurant. Fortunately for foreigners, many restaurants also have plastic models of their menu offerings in a window display. These models make it easy to see what the restaurant offers, and if you see something in the window that appeals to you, you just go inside, sit down, and order. The added advantage of the food displays for foreigners is if you can't read the menu or speak a word of Japanese, you can point to the display of the plastic menu items, indicating to the server what you want.

(A few years ago, I saw a documentary on how these plastic food models are made. It's a fascinating art form! Search online and watch some videos!)

I wanted to take my family to an *unagi* restaurant. Tomoko and I spotted one, and I led my family up to the window display, telling them, "There's another type of food I want you to try because I know you will like it."

As we stood in front of the window, I pointed to all of the options and said I would recommend *unadon*. When they asked me what they were looking at, I told them that unagi is a type of fish and not to worry: It wasn't pickled or fermented, nor was it fish intestines, just fish meat. I assured them that unadon was a bowl of rice with the fish and sauce on top. They trusted me, and we went inside.

Tomoko and I ordered for my family. Everyone was getting the same meal: unadon. The only hiccup was that in Japanese restaurants, the servers bring chopsticks, not forks, and eating rice with chopsticks isn't exactly easy for anyone who isn't comfortable with them. By this time, I had taken my family to a few restaurants, and my mom and aunt quickly realized that they were out of luck as far as eating with a fork was concerned. They had outsmarted me on this issue, though, when we had gotten some fast food that came with plastic cutlery. They had saved the plastic forks, washed them, and proceeded to carry them in their purses for the duration of their stay in Japan. Sure enough, when the unadon came to our table, my mom and aunt whipped the plastic forks out of their purses and used them for eating their lunch. It's pretty much impossible to embarrass me, and more than anything, I wanted them to enjoy their time—including their meals—in Japan, so I just laughed it off. The staff at the restaurant were rather amused, as well.

They loved the unadon, as I knew they would. As Mom and Auntie Darlene were cleaning off their forks and putting them back into their purses, they asked me again, "What kind of fish is this?"

I fessed up. "It's eel."

They weren't upset that I had tricked them, but they did admit that had I been upfront with them, they might have been hesitant to try it and therefore missed out on an excellent meal.

From Ōsaka and Kyōto, we took the shinkansen further south, venturing to a part of Japan I had not yet visited: Kyūshū, the south island,[51] where Nagasaki is located. In addition to travelling around Asia, I had made it a goal to see as much of Japan as I could while I was living there. Taking my family as far south as Nagasaki and Hiroshima was a bit self-serving, but they were definitely interested because, of course, of the historical significance of these cities.

My school had a Wellness Club in Aso, one of the main cities on Kyūshū. We had booked rooms there ahead of time, so that was our home while we stayed in that area. The Aso Wellness Club had tatami rooms, like the one in Tateshina where Ken and I had stayed. Since I had no beds in my apartment, my family slept on the floor every night during their stay in Japan. The Wellness Club, like many Japanese homes, also had *shōji*[52] walls and sliding shōji doors. Shōji is fairly thick and strong, but it *is* paper, so it doesn't withstand being punched or punctured. Somewhere along the way, my aunt nudged her suitcase a little too closely and forcefully against the wall in the room we were sleeping in, resulting in about a two-inch tear in the shōji. She felt bad, but there was nothing we could do about it. Well, that is, until she produced a roll of scotch tape from her purse and patched it up as best she could. I started to wonder what the heck else she was carrying around in that magical purse of hers.

From our Wellness Club, we took a day trip to Mount Aso, the largest active volcano in Japan, where we were met by steaming geysers and that awful rotten-egg sulfur smell. The geography of and around Mount Aso is beautiful, with wide, expansive valleys and volcanic rock.

---

[51] Japan has four main islands: Honshū, the biggest, where Tōkyō, Ōsaka, and Kyōto are located; Hokkaidō, the northernmost island; Shikoku, south of Honshū's most western tip; and Kyūshū, south and slightly west of Honshū.

[52] Shoji: thick white paper used in walls and doors, traditionally made of wood fibers

We stayed long enough to take some pictures, do a bit of walking, and start getting headaches from the stinky, steaming bursts of sulfur.

From Aso, we headed to Nagasaki, where one of my students was from, for a day trip. Yoko was a schoolteacher living and teaching in Fujisawa. She was a gentle, kind, lovely woman with whom I always had interesting conversations about teaching and Japan. Yoko was home at her parents' place for Golden Week and when she heard my family was coming to visit, she was gracious enough to offer to be our tour guide around Nagasaki for the day. We spent most of the day at Huis Ten Bosch, a theme park of sorts depicting Dutch buildings, canals, gardens, and even a windmill. Until Yoko introduced us to this park, I had no idea that Dutch influence and relations were significant to that part of Japan.

When we finished touring around the Aso area, we started to make our way back home. On the way, we stopped for a couple of days in Hiroshima, a city everyone knows about for its place in history. Hiroshima is on Honshū, the island north of Kyūshū, and was on our route back to the Tōkyō area. We started by going to the Hiroshima Peace Memorial Park to see the remnants of Genbaku Dome, one of the only buildings still partially standing after the bombing. This dome was designated as a UNESCO World Heritage site in 1996. From there, we continued to the Hiroshima Peace Memorial Museum.

I'm not a big fan of museums in general; I get bored quickly. I'd much rather be outdoors exploring the geography, architecture, and monuments such as the Great Wall of China, the Pyramids of Egypt, and Mount Fuji. As much as I love archaeology and history, looking at artifacts behind glass and reading about them is, for some reason, completely uninteresting for me. I usually last about an hour at most in a museum.

There are, however, several museums that have been and still are on my "must visit" list. These include the Cairo Museum (a person really must see King Tut's headpiece with their own eyes!) and other museums of significance. The museum in Hiroshima is one of those must-sees.

These days, it's possible to take a virtual tour of the museum, but at that time, I hadn't even seen pictures of the displays, so I didn't know what to expect. The museum is tastefully done, but it doesn't hide the horror of what happened on that day so many years ago. For many of us, August 6, 1945, is a date forever attached to an event that we learned about in school. The museum, however, brings the event to life, displaying artifacts that survived the bombing and telling personal stories of people who had no idea why the sky was suddenly imploding upon them. I was horrified by the stories of adults who had been working in their gardens or children who were playing outside and suddenly saw a flash in the sky, not knowing what had happened. Their confusion and horror were amplified minutes later as they saw their bodies suddenly shedding skin as if their arms were covered by the dried skin of an onion.

By the time we walked down the final corridor and exited the building, I had tears streaming down my face. This museum did not bore me.

Finish Line

My family left Japan in early May 1994, and by that time, I was two months into my third year there. My childhood dream of becoming a teacher and then teaching in another country had been a reality for two years. But right around the time my family left Japan, so did my friends.

Teresa, Ken, Mark, Stephen, Michelle. All of us had come to Japan having signed a two-year contract. And most of my friends, like me, stayed for a third year, but some left after that two-year commitment had ended. Teresa, Ken, and Stephen had all arrived before I did, so the third year of their contract expired while I was still only partially through mine. Ken stayed for a fourth year, but after three years of working in Fujisawa, he requested a transfer to a different school, and so I lost my closest co-worker. While he wasn't placed terribly far away, I missed seeing him every day. He had been one of my constants since I arrived at Narita. Teresa and Stephen left after their third year, and for me, that meant the hub of our wheel was broken. Teresa was one of my two anchors outside of school (Mark was the other), and not having those weekly gatherings at her apartment left a huge void in my social life. Michelle had arrived five months after I had and left after two years, so I was part of organizing both her welcome and farewell parties.

New teachers started arriving to replace those who had left. Over the next two decades of my teaching career in Canada, training and mentoring new teachers and student teachers became one of my favourite professional duties. Helping these new arrivals to Japan learn some of the lessons I had learned (discerning which train is the right train, knowing that putting soy sauce on your rice is an unforgivable sin) was rewarding and fun.

But my social life was taking a huge hit. I couldn't relate to these new teachers. I have always compared this dynamic to being a grade 12 student who is surrounded by grade 10 students. They had the wet-behind-the-ears naïveté and excitement that I'd had in my first several months, but I was well past that stage. While I could remember what it felt like to be excited and intrigued by a new culture, I couldn't relate to them. I wasn't a clueless foreigner anymore. I wasn't excited by every new part of Japanese culture, and I had seen all of the must-see sights new arrivals were eager to visit, some of them multiple times. It had all become routine to me.

Yet I also wasn't a local, and I never would be. Over the summer of 1994, I started to feel more foreign than I had felt at any point in Japan. Japan is an easy place to live because it's safe and the people are gracious and polite, but outsiders will always be exactly that. As an island nation, Japan has a strong sense of homogeneity. Even Canadians, Americans, Europeans, and the like who are completely fluent in the language and well-accustomed to the culture will always stand out visibly and therefore encounter the barriers that visible minorities in many cultures face.

After adjusting for two years but knowing I would always be viewed as an outsider, and especially when my like-minded friends began leaving, I didn't know where I fit. The new teachers were going out and exploring the places I had explored in my first few months, and my students were living their daily lives, which I was only a part of as their teacher. I was in cultural purgatory.

It became clear that I need to make a decision: Was it time to go home? Or was I prepared to fully commit to this culture and get serious about becoming more fluent in the language so I could make a life in this country? The latter had never been my intention regardless of what country I had ended up in to pursue teaching overseas. The goal had been to do it for a few years, and I was starting to feel that I had done what I had set out to do.

I missed the big, blue Alberta sky (the humidity, haze, and sticky summer heat in Japan and I never agreed with each other). I missed Alberta beef. I missed being able to go to the doctor without having to find someone to translate for me. And I missed my family and friends back home more than I had in the first two years, probably because I now had a void in my social life.

In my first year, one of my great aunties died. She had always been like a third grandmother to me, and I will always regret that I wasn't able to attend her funeral. About that time, one of my cousins got married to a woman I had gone to university with, and they had asked me to emcee their wedding. I couldn't because I hadn't earned enough holiday time yet. (They married four months after I moved to Japan.) I had also missed the wedding of another good friend from university who had asked me to be a bridesmaid.

Friends and family back home were moving on with their lives, getting married, having children, moving away, dying. I didn't want to miss any more of my Canadian life.

It was time to go home.

CHAPTER 9

ALBERTA BOUND

When I signed away two years of my life in August of 1991, I was a naive, twenty-one-year-old farm girl who had lived in a "big city" of 60,000 people for four years while earning my teaching degree. As a twenty-two-year-old, I trustingly hopped on a plane with a mountain of luggage, ready to take on the world and let the world show me what it had to offer. Now, at twenty-five, I was more mature, I had had my first professional job, and I had proven to myself that I had what it took to work and live in a foreign country. I needed to start winding down my life in Japan and prepare for my new Canadian life.

My contract ended on March 3, 1995, but seven months earlier, when Michelle left after her two years were up, I had decided I was going to finish out my contract and then head back home.

But then what?

I had, at the ripe old age of twenty-five, fulfilled every dream I'd ever had for myself, other than those items on my "Fifty Things to Do Before I Die" list that Colleen had me make on my initial flight to Japan. But the items on that list were things like writing a book, buying a house, travelling to 100 countries, and other big-ticket dreams. Those were great goals to have, but how the heck would I create a bridge between where I was and where I could do those kinds of things? I needed a job, a place to live, a foundation on which I could settle myself while working toward checking those other life goals off the list. The future was so open and so empty that it terrified me.

I had a teaching degree, and by the time I left Japan, I would have three years' experience teaching ESL in Japan. My teaching experience became my new anchor point. I decided that since I loved what I had been doing in Japan, I should look for opportunities to teach ESL in Canada.

In the fall of 1991 while waiting for my work visa to be approved, I had asked to meet with the ESL program coordinator at my university to pick his brain and get a sense of what I was getting myself into by moving to Japan. When I was considering submitting my resignation, I decided to take a week-long holiday in October 1994 (by this time, I had three weeks' vacation time instead of two) to go home and get a sense of the ESL landscape in Canada. While back, I again invited myself to meet with the ESL coordinator and get some information about ESL opportunities in Canada. He was, again, helpful and generous with his time. By the time I left for Japan again, I had with me an application package for the University of Calgary's ESL Diploma Program—a one-year program with a heavy focus on second language learning, linguistics, and ESL curriculum design and teaching. Back in Japan, I had a lot of paperwork to do: namely, my application for the diploma program ... and my resignation letter.

Christmas Cake

My company required three months' notice of a resignation so that it had time to find a replacement and secure their work visa. So at the end of October, I wrote and submitted my resignation, notifying my school that I would not be renewing my contract when it ended on March 3, 1995. Final answer.

My company didn't want us telling our students too far in advance that we were leaving. As a private language school, it was as much of a business as it was a school, if not more so. When students learned that the teacher they had grown fond of was leaving them forever, a certain amount of attrition always occurred. Students cancelled or simply didn't renew their lesson contracts. Others requested to be placed with one of the teachers currently in the school for fear they would not like their teacher's replacement. I am vehemently opposed to lying to and misleading people, so while I didn't offer up to students far in advance that I was leaving, if they asked, I told them honestly what my intentions were.

Of course, they were disappointed to hear that I was leaving, and I knew that I would miss them as much as they missed me. But as I began announcing to my students my plans to return to Canada, an interesting conversation transpired—one that I hadn't anticipated.

After living in Japan for almost three years, there was still at least one cultural lesson I hadn't yet learned. I was twenty-five, and I was headed home. My students started to quiz me on *why* I was going home. I told them that it was because I had intended to stay two or three years, and I felt it was time to go home. They weren't satisfied. They proceeded to push a little more, with a smile on their faces that I didn't understand.

"Will you get married?" they started to ask me.

"Well, maybe eventually," I answered innocently. "I don't know. Maybe someday."

"But that is why you are going back to Canada: to get married," they *informed* me.

"No, I'm going to be going back to university and then looking for jobs teaching ESL in Canada," I clarified.

They weren't convinced.

They were trying to get me to admit that I was going home to get married. Which I definitely was not.

"But you are twenty-five," they told me.

"Yes?" I answered. I had no idea what my age had to do with my decision to move on to the next phase of my life.

And then they explained.

Christmas cake is a term used in Japan to describe a woman of twenty-five years or older who is not married. The label comes from the fact that Christmas cake is tasty, desirable, and fresh up until December 25, but after Christmas, it is considered leftover, stale, and undesirable. Women of twenty-six and older are past their prime and therefore less eligible for marriage. If a woman wants to have great options for a husband, she has to get married by twenty-five; otherwise, fewer men will want her.

They figured I was going home to find a husband before my options started running out. I was, in their minds, Christmas cake …

Banana and Egg

... which I thoroughly enjoyed eating when I went home to Canada again at Christmastime in 1994. It was my first time returning home for Christmas with my family in three years—and my second time going home in a little over two months. It might seem odd on the surface that I spent so much money and used my vacation days for going home twice within a couple of months when I was returning for good only two months later. But the trips home in October and December were functional: I had to do some legwork for my future. (Remember, this was before the Internet.) Going home when I did also provided me the opportunity to take home my summer clothes and other belongings I wouldn't need for my last two months in Japan. Of course, after almost three years, I had accumulated a lot of possessions. Many of my goods wouldn't be coming home with me, but a considerable amount would be. I started the migration of those belongings on the two trips home so I wouldn't have an unreasonable amount of luggage when I went back for good.

Shortly after I returned from my Christmas trip home, I was chatting on the phone with Michelle No. 1, the teacher I had replaced. She mostly stayed at home since relinquishing her position at my school. She did, however, teach a few hours of private lessons on the side each week to make a bit of extra money and give herself something to do other than tending the home. She had a student she wanted me to meet.

"He's really sweet," she informed me. "I think you would like him. He's looking for a Canadian or American girlfriend."

"But I'm going home in about six weeks," I clarified. "There's no point in meeting him, or anyone new, for that matter. I'm winding things down and wrapping things up here, not starting anything new."

"But you never know!" she insisted. "You need to give this a chance."

"I've never been on a blind date in my life, and I have no desire to start now," I insisted. "Plus, I've already submitted my resignation."

"But you may end up like me! Look at me. I married a Japanese man and stayed here." She kept pushing to try and set me up with this guy. "Just meet him for dinner. My husband and I will come with you. Would that make things more comfortable for you?"

Because she wouldn't take no for an answer, I finally relented so I could get her off my back. But I emphasized that the only reason I was agreeing was that she and Makoto would be there, as well. If they didn't come, the deal was off.

She got back to me a couple of days later with the date and time. She told me we would all meet across the street from my school, which was close to the train station and therefore handy for her husband coming back from work. It was also near a lot of good restaurants.

The dreaded evening arrived. But I had agreed to this arrangement, and I wasn't going to go back on my word, so I set out for the meeting spot, determined to be on my best behaviour. Michelle arrived shortly after I did.

"Makoto can't come," she dropped on me as soon as she showed up. "He has to work late, so I will leave the two of you alone."

"But the deal was that I wasn't taking part in this unless you two come, too," I argued.

"I will stay until he shows up to make the introduction," she said.

I was furious, but it was too late for me to do anything. The guy arrived right at that moment before I had a chance to tell her the deal was off and leave.

As promised, she introduced us and then promptly left me alone with him, in exactly the situation I had told her I refused to be in. Despite my anger, I had to put a smile on my face since he was standing in front of me and I didn't want to look like a complete jerk. As much as I wanted to, I couldn't leave. To do so would have been extremely rude, and for all I knew, he was quite possibly a really terrific guy. I didn't want to be mean. It was one evening of my life, so I resigned myself to going and being pleasant.

We exchanged hellos and he immediately told me he had a restaurant in mind. I followed him to what was a pretty upscale American-style restaurant with a menu comparable to what you would find in a decent restaurant in Canada or the US. Obviously, he was trying to cater to me, and I didn't want to come across as ungrateful even though I would have preferred a nice Japanese restaurant.

The food was terrific; the conversation, torturous. He was completely polite and friendly. I just didn't want to be there, and the more we talked, the more I realized I definitely didn't want to see him ever again.

Not because he was anything but gracious, but because we were oil and water.

"Do you like karaoke?" he asked me.

I loved it. Music has always been a big part of my life, and karaoke had become one of my favourite past times over the previous thirty-four months. It was a fun, inexpensive, and enjoyable way to spend time doing something I love (and am good at) with fun friends who also loved it. He hated it.

"Japanese people love golf, but I hate golf," he proclaimed.

"Athletic" is definitely a word I would never use to describe myself, but in my time in Japan, I had learned how to play golf a little. Going to the driving range is a favourite weekend activity in Japan. Hirata-san, the lovely squid-guts man who wasn't even my student, had taken me to the driving range several times to teach me his favourite pastime. To this day, I still haven't played a full eighteen holes. (I did play a round of nine-hole golf with Ken and Stephen on the Saipan trip, beating them both soundly, but that's as much time as I've spent on an actual course.) Even so, I had enjoyed learning how to play golf. It, too, was a fun way to spend time with friends on the weekends.

With every topic of conversation this poor fellow brought up, it became clearer and clearer that we had completely opposite interests, and finding things to talk about grew increasingly more difficult. We had *nothing* in common. In fact, I started to feel like I was more Japanese than he was (or more than he was trying to be). It became apparent that he was trying to become Americanized.

There are two metaphors in Japan for describing Asians and Caucasians: a person called an *egg* is yellow on the inside but white on the outside, and a *banana* is the opposite—yellow on the outside but white on the inside. I had never thought of myself as having "become Japanese," but I did try for three years to fit in and to embrace the culture of the temporary home I had chosen. This fellow expressed how he spent a lot of time with American soldiers from the nearby military base and loved American culture. That was the draw for wanting to meet me—that I was Canadian. He didn't want a Japanese wife. He wanted someone from Canada or the US. I was an egg, and he was a banana.

During the Q & A session with him, I had a revelation. That evening brought full circle my having spent almost three years struggling for an answer when my students consistently asked, "What's a typical Canadian food?" "What do Canadians like to do for hobbies?" "What's a typical Canadian __________?" There is no answer except a long one. My answers were always prefaced with, "It depends on which part of Canada you are from, but also on where your ancestors are from, and ... and ... and ... and."

"In my part of the country, we eat a lot of beef because that's one of the main industries, but on the east and west coasts of Canada, people eat a lot of seafood."

"My hobbies? I like hiking and riding horses and skiing, but everyone is different."

I had spent three years trying to explain to people from a largely homogeneous culture—where "everyone plays golf" and "everyone likes karaoke"—what it is like to be part of a cultural mosaic. You cannot understand those differences until you live on the other side and experience them for yourself. And he didn't see that I was not like his army buddies. I was a woman who couldn't be fully defined in a couple of sentences, even in the context of my own nationality, because my country's collective national identity is complex and varied. It encompasses so much more than hockey, Tim Horton's, and beavers. And I certainly had NO concept of what it was like to be part of the US military life. He one-upped me in that department.

We finished our meal, and I started to look for an opportunity to extract myself from the evening. After he paid the bill, he asked for my phone number, which I politely declined to give to him. I thanked him for the nice meal and wished him well.

Any doubt about staying in Japan that Michelle had hoped would be planted within me was simply not there. I was going home in six weeks.

I Will Never Forget You

Preparing to return to Canada involved an entirely different mindset than getting ready to move to Japan. I felt a similar type of excitement within me, but there were also significant differences.

First and foremost, I knew what I would be stepping into upon returning home. I had, in the past several months, started to tell myself that to continue teaching ESL in Canada, I would likely have to move to Toronto or Vancouver. The immigrant and international student populations in those cities were much higher than they were in Alberta. But before doing that, I was going back to school in Calgary, two hours from where I had grown up and two hours in a different direction from where I had completed my education degree. I was looking forward to being home again for a good chunk of time before worrying about future employment.

I was also starting to try and come to terms with the fact that, unlike moving to Japan, which was temporary and an adventure, moving back home meant settling into "real life." It could be a long time before I saw some of these people I had grown to love over the past three years. There was a chance I would never see them again. I was genuinely and deeply fond of every one of my students, and I realized I had not just been their teacher. I had become a representative of my country and culture, and they of theirs. And I considered many of them friends. I had to start saying goodbye to them.

Of course, my Saturday Night Fever class planned a party, as did some of my other group classes on different nights. There were farewell parties for me every night during the last two weeks that I was in Japan, so I had to schedule in time over the weekends and in the mornings for packing and getting my life wrapped up. My private students didn't know any of my other students, so there were no parties with the former, but some of them wanted to take me out for lunch or dinner. Those who didn't brought me gifts. A lot of gifts.

Gift giving is a huge part of Japanese culture. When a Japanese person travels abroad, they are expected to bring back treats for their co-workers and family members. On Valentine's Day, women give chocolate to all of the men in their lives: co-workers, friends, family members, classmates. And White Day, exactly one month later, is when men return the favour, giving candy or other gifts to the girls or women who had given them chocolate the month prior. I had known about the importance of gift giving when I arrived in Japan and had brought maple cookies and candies for all of my classes when I arrived. Now I was to receive.

For most of my last year, I had a student named Yukiko. Yukiko was registered in a semi-private class, which meant there could be one, two, or three people in the class. Fortunately for her, no one else ever registered for her time slot, so for the price of a semi-private lesson, she got a private lesson with me. Yukiko was, of course, polite, but she was painfully shy and self-conscious of her broken English. Even though I was never judgemental and made a point of always being positive and encouraging with my students, she was clearly embarrassed to speak. Even after several months, I had to work hard to get her to say much during her lesson. She was so extremely shy—and I was still young and not completely self-confident—that I was never completely sure if she liked me. I feared part of her hesitancy to speak was that she disliked me, so her classes were always filled with a bit of tentativeness on both our parts.

In my last class with her, she proved I couldn't have been further from the truth regarding how she felt about me.

Yukiko arrived for her last class with a box and put it on the floor beside her. Because of the tradition of gift giving, I knew this was a gift for me, but I ignored it and proceeded with the lesson. At the end of our session, she paused in her seat for a moment, silently looking at me. It was a little awkward, but I smiled, and then she reached down for the box. As she handed it to me, she explained carefully and slowly, in her best English, that she wanted to give this gift to me because she was so appreciative of my helping her with her English over the past several months. As I took the box from her, she again went silent and waited.

She remained silent, watching me as I removed the lid, looked inside, and gasped. I pulled out a stunning Japanese doll with a porcelain face wearing a peach-coloured silk kimono.

"My grandmother made this doll. And it is very special, and so I wanted to give it to you."

It was my turn to be speechless. I was holding in my hands a twelve-inch-high doll that, in a store, I was sure would have had a price tag of several hundred dollars attached to it. But this doll would never be found in a store. And it was priceless. Her grandmother had made it. Surely, it was important to Yukiko. And she was gifting it to me. I realized she didn't dislike me after all.

In the years since I have been back in Canada, I've seen news footage of house fires where people lose everything. I have often thought, *What would I grab to take with me if my house were on fire and I had to quickly run outside?* That doll is on the list of my top five items.

Police Report

Even though I took all of my summer clothes and copious other belongings back to Alberta in October and December, I still had a lot of possessions to pack up and either mail back home or take with me in my luggage. I had acquired quite a few books, and I wanted to keep my Japanese language books in particular. Those got packaged up and mailed back to my parents' address via surface mail because it was the cheapest option and I knew I wouldn't be in a hurry for them back home. There were, however, two items I had acquired that posed a problem.

One was my bike, which had served me well. On most summer Sundays, I would use it to ride to the coast and then continue riding on the paved path along the water, spending two to four hours cycling along the beach and into Kamakura. It was great exercise, and it was freeing to be able to explore places more quickly than walking. For the first year and a half that I had the bike, I would carry it up the three flights of stairs to my apartment every day after coming home and keep it in my apartment. My building was on the corner of two busy streets. There really wasn't anywhere to keep a bike outside unless I tied it to the street pole—which is exactly what I started doing after about a year and a half when I got too lazy to haul it up the stairs. I bought a chain and a lock and started locking my bike to the street pole.

As summer ended and I entered my last six months of work, I started to wonder what I would do with the bike. I had certainly gotten my money's worth out of it, so leaving it behind for the teacher who replaced me would have been reasonable. Still, I thought about selling the bike so I could get some money out of it. I wasn't sure how to go about doing that other than to start spreading the word to other foreign teachers.

When I returned home from work one day by train, I discovered that the problem had been solved for me. The bike was no longer attached to the pole. There was no sign of it or the chain that had secured it.

Despite being in one of the safest countries in the world, I immediately assumed my bike had been stolen, and my instinct was to report it to the police. The nearest police station was a couple of blocks away, so I walked there, entered, and proceeded to explain to them in my best Japanese that my bike had been stolen. My Japanese was still fairly basic, so it took me a few tries to get my message across.

Once the officer realized why I was there, he sat me down and started asking me some questions. I answered them as best I could, and when I thought we were done, he passed a sheet of blank paper to me. I looked at him ... blankly ... and after a bit of back and forth, I figured out that he wanted me to draw a picture of my bike. A picture. Of my bike. Um ... it was a bike.

At this point, I realized I was never going to see my bike again, and that was probably OK. It saved me from the dilemma of what to do with it since I was leaving the country for good. However, in The Land of Supreme Politeness, I knew he was trying to be helpful, so for me to walk out without drawing the picture for him would have been rude.

I scribbled out a picture of a bike, shaded the areas of the frame, and wrote *murasaki* (purple) on the side, adding an arrow pointing to the parts of the frame that were purple.

As I passed him the paper and pen, I smiled widely, bowed while offering a dōmo arigatō gozaimasu, and left.

I never saw him or my bike again.

Problem solved.

Piano Man

I still had my second problematic possession to deal with before leaving the country: a piano. Not a keyboard, a digital piano. The bike problem had resolved itself, and if it hadn't, I likely would have left it for my replacement. The piano was a different story. It was only a couple of years old, and I had paid C$1,000 for it, buying it off of another teacher who was heading back to Canada after using the piano for only a year. Having spent that much money on it only a year prior, I didn't want to abandon it in my apartment for someone I didn't know—and who quite possibly wouldn't even know how to play it.

I asked around. No one wanted it. I wasn't terribly surprised, but I had hoped to sell it and recoup some of my money. Instead, I was left with two options: leave it behind or try to take it home.

Of course, I chose the most difficult option.

The piano could be easily taken apart. The legs and bottom panel with the pedals came off, so I detached them, wrapped the whole kit and caboodle up into a blanket—yes, a blanket—and tied the blanket with some string. Then I called on one of my favourite services offered in Japan: luggage delivery to and from Narita Airport. (Obviously, I didn't know about this service when I returned from my first trip back to Canada.) It's a genius idea. Call the company, schedule a day and time for them to pick up your luggage from your home, and retrieve it at the airport long enough to check it in and let the airline worry about it from there.

So when I went home at Christmastime, I planned on taking the piano back with me, along with one other large suitcase that was sufficiently stuffed. The piano would be my second piece of check luggage.

The day before my flight, my doorbell rang and I opened it to find a tiny Japanese man, smaller than me (I am five feet three inches), eagerly awaiting my luggage. Now, let me remind you that this wasn't a keyboard. It was a Korg digital piano with eighty-eight weighted keys, and anyone who has one knows how heavy they are. Standing on its side, the piano was close to being as tall as the man who came to transfer it, and it probably didn't weigh much less than he did, either. In true Japanese fashion, he didn't grumble. He politely took hold of the piano and, huffing and puffing, lugged it down the stairs into his truck.

The next day, I retrieved my piano at the airport and proceeded to the check-in counter, fully anticipating getting a lot of flak for having an oversized, overweight piano as my second piece of "luggage." This was when checking in your luggage was somewhat unpredictable: Sometimes, the agent would charge for an overweight bag; sometimes they wouldn't. Sometimes they would charge for a third bag; sometimes they wouldn't. I was fully prepared to have to pay extra since the piano was so heavy, but the check-in agent didn't even blink. She tagged my piano, and off it went into the guts of the airport, only to be seen again by me once we both arrived back in Canada.

Have I mentioned that Japanese people are SO polite?

Sayōnara[53]

March 3, 1995 was the three-year anniversary of my arrival in Japan. I had to leave the country by that date. Since my work visa expired that day, for me to stay even one day longer would have been illegal. I had arranged to spend five days travelling in the northern part of Thailand with my co-worker, Maya, who had replaced Michelle No.

[53] Sayonara: goodbye

2 the previous August. But because March 3 was a Friday and Maya worked Saturdays, I had to head to Thailand a day before she did, which meant I had two nights and one full day in Thailand by myself before she joined me. Obviously, I didn't want to take all of my belongings with me to Thailand, so I arranged to keep my going-back-to-Canada luggage at Tomoko's house and stay a day in Japan after the trip to Thailand before heading home. (After the trip to Thailand, I would be allowed to enter and stay in Japan on a tourist visa for up to ninety days.)

Off I went to Bangkok. I had decided to stay there since it was the easiest way to connect with Maya and also because I hadn't seen any part of Bangkok when Mark, Stephen, and I had ventured to Thailand. With all of the travel I had done in the past three years, I had hotel points saved up, so I decided to treat myself: I booked a Hilton for two free nights in Bangkok. On my solo day, I hired a private driver to take me to the various tourist attractions around the city and give me a general tour. His English was excellent, as was his customer service, and it was a great way to spend the day decompressing in this in-between time of having left Japan but not yet being home.

When Maya arrived at the airport in Bangkok, I was waiting for her, and we boarded the next flight—taking us to Chiang Mai, in the northern jungle of Thailand. We rode elephants in the jungle; ate great local food; and toured the local temples, markets, and countryside. When leaving our cozy hotel room on our last day, we left a little bit of money on the nightstand as a tip, since we had received great customer service. Before we even got to the front desk to check out, word had gotten back to the front desk clerk that we had left money behind. He looked at us, overly concerned, and told us that the staff had found money on the table in our room. We assured him that yes, it was a tip for the staff, not a test. I think he was worried we would think the staff had stolen our money.

Seeing the north of Thailand and touring Bangkok for the full day left me feeling that I had "done" Thailand. I could happily return to explore some of the other islands in the south, but having been to Ko Phi Phi in the south and Chiang Mai in the north allowed me to check this country off my list.

We flew back to Tōkyō, and I accompanied Maya back to Fujisawa.

I spent one night plus a few hours hanging out at Tomoko's house. She had graciously kept my luggage for me. She and her parents had been so welcoming and kind to me over the previous three years, it seemed fitting to spend my true last hours in Japan with her family. I had said my goodbyes to everyone else. My replacement had arrived. I had gotten to know her a bit, introduced her to my students (soon to be her students), and I had trained her. My students were going to be in good hands; I could tell. There was nothing left for me to do but take a deep breath and wait for my flight home.

Those last few hours with Tomoko's family were quiet and heartwarming. As I left their doorstep one last time, there were tears, deep bows, and hugs. We had shared each other's cultures and adopted one another as a chosen family. Now I was leaving, taking with me their gifts and my memories of a warm, hospitable family, representative of their whole society.

I boarded the train for Narita one last time.

Planes, Trains, and More Planes

My school had given me the money for my return trip ticket. The cash they doled out to teachers who were leaving their jobs—and Japan—was the equivalent of about C$1,500. Even though I'd saved up a good wad of money in my three years working in Japan, I was still a cheap-ass and wanted to squeeze as much out of that $1,500 as I could. So, of course, I booked the cheapest flight back home I could find.

Instead of flying from Tōkyō to Vancouver to Calgary, which would have eaten up almost all of the $1,500 and taken about fourteen hours, I took the milk run. My itinerary took me from Tōkyō to Los Angeles to San Francisco to Spokane to Calgary. Four flights. And then a two-hour drive back to my parents' house once I arrived in Calgary. I had convinced myself that pocketing the leftover $800 was worth the more than thirty hours of travelling.

The flight to Los Angeles was quiet. Most of the passengers were Japanese, and generally, Japanese people are quiet, especially on a long flight. They sleep. I couldn't sleep; I was too full of conflicting emotions. A huge wave of sadness washed over me as we took off from Narita, but as soon as we were at cruising altitude, I started to look ahead, much like I had done several years prior on Jericho Beach in Vancouver. I didn't know exactly what lay ahead of me, but I knew the next, exciting phase of my life was about to begin. I settled in for my last chance at being surrounded by these people who had been so welcoming and fun for the previous three years.

We arrived in Los Angeles on time and departed for San Francisco, also on time. After a short layover, I boarded a northbound plane headed for Spokane. I was getting closer, heading in the direction of Canada. The second and third flights were full of average Americans flying around their country, going about their business, oblivious to the fact that someone among them was "coming home" after a life-changing three years of living in a completely different country. I spoke to no one. Instead, I observed and started making mental adjustments. Although these were Americans, I had more in common with them than I did with the people I had been surrounded by for three years. Yet I felt like an outsider looking in more than I ever had on any other time I had spent in the US. My brain was still in Japanese mode.

By the time I got on my final flight, I was excited but also exhausted. The hop from Spokane to Calgary was short, barely an hour, and it was rowdy. Many of my fellow passengers were middle-aged businessmen from Calgary coming home after spending a few days golfing in Spokane. I still spoke to no one, amusingly noting how, even on a flight, culture can be so distinctly represented, as shown on this flight compared to the quiet trans-Pacific flight full of subdued Japanese people. Obviously, I was not a middle-aged businessman, but these people displayed Albertan culture—a culture that only those of us from here would fully understand. I could have picked these men out of a crowd anywhere in the US and immediately identified them as Albertans. As I looked around the plane and listened to the conversations, I smiled. These were my people, and I was close to home.

We landed on time, and sure enough, as promised, my mom was there waiting to pick me up. In a week, I had gone from Fujisawa to Narita to Bangkok to Chiang Mai to Bangkok to Narita to Fujisawa to Narita to Los Angeles to San Francisco to Spokane to Calgary.

I took one look at my mom and said, "I don't want to see another airport for a very long time. Take me home."

CONCLUSION

Oh, Canada

There were no parties welcoming me home, but two events served as great welcomes.

Within days of getting back, I started calling up friends to reconnect. Karen, one of my long-time friends who lived only ten minutes from my parents, immediately asked if I wanted to attend the Eagles concert in Calgary the following week. She and her husband had an extra ticket, and I had no hesitation saying yes to seeing one of my favourite bands in concert for the first time. Although our seats were in the nosebleeds, and a bit of a throwback to my attending the sumo basho, the concert was a huge highlight for me. We sat on the side of the stage, and we could see the band members high-fiving each other backstage before they went in front of the audience. Eagles songs have always been high on my list of "driving songs," and when I was learning to play guitar as a young teenager, their music was on some of my self-directed curriculum.

I was back home, taking part in real life activities in Canada again. My friends were happy to see me, and I them!

A second trip to Calgary within those first two weeks reinforced for me who I am and where I come from. At that time, the Calgary Stampede organization was still hosting Rodeo Royale, an indoor rodeo held every March on the Stampede Grounds. My mom had won two tickets on the radio, and since my dad was busy with calves being born, she took me. As soon as we arrived at the venue, we stopped at the concession and grabbed some burgers and drinks since we had driven straight from home and didn't have time to eat anywhere along the way. We got to our seats moments before the rodeo was about to start. Just as I opened my burger to start eating it, the announcer requested that everyone stand for the national anthem. We obeyed, and as I stood there, grease dripping from my burger onto my shoe, out on his white horse in a ten-gallon hat rode Ian Tyson, singing our national anthem. It doesn't get much more cowboy or Albertan than that. I started bawling. It was good to be home.

Not So Fast

Six weeks after I returned home, I got my wisdom teeth taken out. They had been bothering me more and more for several months. Knowing I was coming home, though, I decided to wait and get them dealt with in Canada so I could at least understand what the process involved and talk to the dentist myself. I had an appointment with my hometown dentist, who took one of them out but had to break the tooth in half to do so because they were so impacted. After half an hour of huffing and puffing and wrestling and working up a sweat, he got the one tooth out and promptly announced, "I'm sending you to Calgary for the other three." My dentist fired me!

I got the other three done all at once and spent the next couple of weeks in great pain with my face puffed out, eating Jell-O and soup.

By the time I had healed, it was late April and I started to think about finding a summer job to make some money before starting university in September. I took a job teaching ESL to a young girl two days a week in Calgary. I commuted from my parents' place two hours away and crashed on a friend's couch on the three nights in a row that I needed to be in the city.

After about three weeks of that, and right around the time I got sick of the inconvenience of it, the girl stopped showing up for her lessons—and I also got a phone call at my parents' place from Tōkyō. It was the head office of the language school I had worked for. Would I be available and interested in going back to Japan for three months to work as a substitute teacher in whichever school(s) they would send me to? They would pay for my flights there and back, provide me with accommodation, and pay me the same salary as what I had been making when I left.

It was an easy decision. The perfect summer job had landed in my lap.

OK, Japan is not huge when you are from Canada, the US, or Australia. In comparison, it's pretty tiny. You could fit twenty-six Japans inside Canada. Alberta alone is 75 per cent larger than Japan.[54] But still, it would take twelve hours by shinkansen to travel from the north end of the country to the south end.

Out of all the places in the entire country it could have sent me, my language school placed me in a school fifteen minutes away from where I had been teaching for three years. I was to begin my substitute teaching in the next town over from Fujisawa—Hiratsuka, the town where Michelle No. 1 had settled once she got married. And she was

[54] MapFight.zyx, "Alberta (Canada) is 1.75 times as big as Japan," accessed November 6, 2021 from mapfight.xyz/compare/alberta-vs-jp/

still living there. One of the other two foreign teachers at the Hiratsuka school was a young woman from Calgary named Teresa (not to be confused with Oregonian Teresa) who became and still is a great friend. Considering I had to unexpectedly return to Japan and teach for two months in a school fifteen minutes from where I had lived for three years to meet someone from my stomping grounds, our friendship seemed to have been preordained.

When I had received the call from Tōkyō at my parents' place, the manager told me I could expect to be sent anywhere in Japan and would be at one particular school for a minimum of one week. I could potentially be moving around anywhere in the country on a weekly basis. My stint in Hiratsuka lasted two of the agreed-upon three months. All of the students who had thrown farewell parties for me only weeks prior were surprised and bewildered, but happy, to see me back. I made it clear that I may only be in that neck of the woods for a week or two. But in the two months I was in Hiratsuka, I got to spend time with the friends I had left behind and thought I may never see again, or at least not for years.

And then my situation got even more bizarre. I was moved to a different school for the last month of my commitment. As a substitute teacher, I was living in the apartments that the language school held the leases for. Each teaching position was attached to a specific apartment, so the teacher who replaced me was now living in my former apartment, and so on. Turned out that the teacher who had replaced "my first Teresa," the one from Oregon, hadn't worked out and left only one year into his two-year contract. I was sent to live in Teresa's apartment and to teach her students at her former school. I already knew some of her students. Fortunately, the guy whose school bag I had barfed in was no longer taking English lessons (I could just imagine that reunion!), and I knew most of the other teachers who were working at her school. Her co-worker Jason had been there forever.

"Being" Teresa, teaching her students, and living in the apartment I had spent so much time in was an odd mix of welcomed familiarity and sadness for the good times that were in my rear-view mirror. The apartment felt empty without her, but it was comforting that the last place I lived in Japan was my friend's party pad. It had, after all, been my second home for almost three years.

After my three-month stint was up, I headed back to Calgary, this time, truly for good. Oddly, since then, every job I have had except one has had the same false ending: I resigned from several teaching positions only to be asked to come back for part-time or temporary work. It's become an odd but welcome, unintentional tradition, allowing me to make the transition from one great job to another a little more gradually, a little more easily.

Still, letting go isn't easy.

AFTERWORD

Battle Scar

Every time I look at my left hand, I see it. The tiny, white, crescent-moon-shaped scar perfectly centered, as if it were an intentional tattoo, between the lower knuckle and finger joint on my middle finger. It is a faint reminder of the life-changing decision I made as a naive twenty-one-year-old to uproot myself and commit to living in Japan for a minimum of two years.

The vicious bite of my mailbox in Japan. On one of the 1,095 days I lived in Japan, while hurriedly reaching in to grab my mail, the sharp metal edge of the box decided to lash out at me for some reason. It cut me fiercely on the middle finger of my left hand.

That day was roughly halfway through what ended up being a three-year stay in Japan, and I knew there were letters from home waiting in my mailbox. Although I had been in Japan long enough to push through the roller coaster of emotions that come mainly in the first year of living abroad, I was still desperately missing home. One of the constants in my life was my excitement any time I hurriedly reached into my mailbox to grab the small, puffy, rectangular envelopes that were undoubtedly letters from Canada.

I have never felt so alone as I did for periods of time between 1992 and 1995, living in the suburbs of Tōkyō. Surrounded by millions of people my height, shoulder to shoulder, I was lonelier than I would have been on the moon—homesick for the big, blue Alberta sky and for familiarity. I always describe living in Japan as the best experience of my life. Still, constantly and relentlessly bumping up against cultural differences and misunderstandings is exhausting, frustrating, discouraging, and at times, even depressing. I felt childlike since I was almost illiterate in a country where, ironically, I was working at my first career-related job teaching my own language. My illiteracy, my disconnect from the local culture, and the bite of that mailbox were humbling experiences. When my mailbox lashed out at me, brief as the bite was, I thought the bleeding would never stop. And it hurt like hell! A tiny bite, but giant pain. Simply because I had reached inside too quickly.

"Slow down," higher powers were telling me. "Let go of your past a little, and don't worry about the future. Live in the present and enjoy your now." I've always had the tendency to look and charge ahead. In fact, Ken often said to me during my three years in Japan, "Be where you are."

As difficult as living in Japan was at times, it is also the period of my life that I value the most. Living in a culture where I was both physically and ideologically different offered me rich learning opportunities, especially about myself. The three years I spent teaching abroad have continued to open doors for me that I would have otherwise never even noticed much less walked through.

The scar on my finger is faint, but the memory of my mailbox's brief attack is vivid. That scar serves as a permanent reminder any time I get frustrated and discouraged that my life, compared to most, is good. Really, really good. Perhaps this little nick on my skin remains to nudge me to remember that whenever I make a choice, it is the right choice—and in spite of bumps and roadblocks, I will overcome.

You're Speaking My Language

One of the most common questions I still get from people as soon as I tell them I lived in Japan for three years is, "Are you fluent in Japanese?" Far from it.

I regret that I'm not fluent in any language other than English, even though I have a strong background in linguistics and second language learning. I've spent thousands of hours over the years helping people learn English and helping native speakers of English improve their writing skills, but in the process, I have done myself a great disservice.

I have studied Japanese and German enough to be functional, and I aim to pick up a few useful phrases anytime I travel to a place with a new language. *Shukran jazeelan* (thank you very much) served me well in Egypt! However, I spent much of my time in Japan teaching English—and after work hours, I hung out with fellow Canadians, Americans, or Japanese students and co-workers who wanted to practice their English. For these reasons, I was never truly immersed in the language enough to get a strong handle on it. (And let's be honest: communicating with my students in English was SO much easier than trying to fumble through a conversation forcing them to endure my Japanese.) In fact, after our first year in Japan, Ken and I started to comment to each other about how we were forgetting English because we spent so much of our time using simpler vocabulary so that our students could understand us. There came a point where he and I shamefully admitted we were no longer fluent in any language. Indeed, when I moved back to Canada, I found I had to consciously search for higher-level vocabulary that would have previously come naturally to me.

I took Japanese lessons for four months before leaving Canada, and those were hours well spent, as I had a handle on the basics before I arrived. I also continued taking lessons the whole time I lived there. My school paid for us to have a one-hour lesson every week, and Tomoko was my teacher. I loved her lessons, but at times, my brain got so saturated with all of the language and cultural learning I was doing, I needed a break. My TV service provided me with only basic channels, but I got a lot of Japanese game shows, news programs, and other TV shows. Sometimes I would try to watch them and see how much I could understand. There were frequent occasions, though, when I would switch my TV to *Sesame Street* because my brain needed to refresh itself and function in English, and that was the only English TV program I got.

Going out to movies was doubly entertaining. The most recent releases were subtitled, and subtitled movies were released much earlier than the ones dubbed over in Japanese, so being able to watch a movie in English just as I would back home was also a relief for my brain. The second layer of entertainment kicked in because I'd be the only person (or one of few people) in the movie theatre who understood the jokes in real time. I got used to being the only person laughing in a movie theatre when jokes in English either showed up in the subtitles on a bit of a delay or didn't even come through the translation at all. Recent releases came to Japan only a few weeks after they were released in Canada and the US, so I was able to see movies such as *Schindler's List* and *Aladdin* around the same time friends back home were viewing and talking about them.

Even though my brain was saturated at times, I loved learning Japanese. The pronunciation is fairly simple even though some of the syllables are a little tricky. I loved the feeling of the pure vowel sounds rolling off my tongue and feeling the shape of my mouth that is required to pronounce Japanese sounds correctly in the front of the mouth. They're less guttural than the pronunciations we have in English.

I also found the writing system utterly fascinating. To me, the three different scripts were not intimidating at all. Instead, I approached them as I would a jigsaw puzzle and was excited to start building words once I knew the meanings of different kanji and kana. This learning took me back to the mindset of a child, and I began to remember when I first learned to read and write English in school. The same feelings of excitement and accomplishment came over me as I became more literate in Japan.

There was a fairly plump, pleasant, middle-aged lady working at a newsstand half a block from my school, and she was my source of postage stamps the whole time I lived in Japan. She was a lovely, grandmotherly type lady, and being able to talk to her more and more as my stay extended was satisfying and exciting. I could tell, too, she was pleased to be able to talk to me more as time went on, as she didn't speak a word of English. Probably in my first visit to her newsstand, I had told her I was from Canada and teaching at the language school down the street. Toward the end of my stay, I was delighted to be able to tell her more about myself, my country, and the family and friends on the receiving end of all of the stamps she had sold me over the years. Saying goodbye to her before I left was a sad moment.

My favourite method of learning, though, was karaoke. My students, expat friends, and I spent a lot of money on karaoke over those years, and at first, I was too shy to sing in front of other people. Once I broke through that barrier by cheating and sticking to only songs I knew would make me sound good, I started trying a wider variety of English songs. The karaoke studios all had a vast selection of both English and Japanese songs. As I began to notice and applaud my students' attempts at singing in English, I realized that karaoke offered a terrific language learning opportunity, and I began learning and singing some of my favourite Japanese songs from the radio. Of course, my students went wild and were honoured and impressed at my efforts. Once I reached this point of enlightenment, I realized that singing, watching movies and TV, and reading aloud were great ways to practice pronunciation and listening skills and pick up new vocabulary. These tricks became part of my teaching advice for the rest of my ESL career in Japan and Canada.

At one point, about a year and a half into my stay, I also started studying German again. I had studied it in high school, wanted to continue learning it, and needed to do something with my brain that didn't involve further saturating it with Japanese culture and language. I took German lessons for a few months until I got a little impatient with my teacher, who was from Germany but spent most of the lesson making small talk with me in English.

Perhaps the most linguistically gratifying moment I had in Japan was when, after I had lived there for several months, I decided I was brave enough to pick up the phone and try to order a pizza. One night, I didn't feel like cooking, nor did I feel like going out, and the little convenience store on the ground floor of my building had lots of snacks, but I wanted a pizza. A good pizza. And I knew where I wanted to get it from, but I didn't feel like walking to the pizza place. I rehearsed my order in my mind several times before taking a deep breath, picking up the phone, and calling in my order. I wasn't 100 per cent clear on all of the questions they were asking me, but I knew what to say when ordering a pizza. Size, type of pizza, name, address, phone number. Instead of fretting over whether I was answering them correctly, I charged on, giving them all of the information I knew I needed to provide in such a circumstance. I knew there were a few questions that I was completely ignoring or answering incorrectly, but in the end, I got my message across. The phone call ended, and half an hour later, exactly what I wanted appeared at my door.

This breakthrough not only opened up more options for feeding myself, but it gave me a needed confidence boost that pushed me further along in being brave, trying to express myself, and not worrying about doing so perfectly. The main goal was to get my message across, and this is another point I then stressed to my own students for years to come: Do not be afraid to make mistakes. Try, and even if you're not speaking perfectly, you will find success. It's great advice for *any* aspect of life.

Superstar

My three years in Japan was the first and most significant amount of time I had spent anywhere as a visible minority. At first, the pseudo-celebrity status was a bit of an ego trip. Everywhere I went, people wanted to talk to me, whether to practice their English or to learn something first-hand about Canada or the US. Most locals assumed I was American, and as soon as I corrected them, they showed even more intrigue. Canada does not infiltrate the movie and TV screens and radio airwaves nearly to the extent that US culture and pop culture does, and many people knew little about Canada.

The superstar status, though, gets annoying to expats at times after the novelty wears off and they simply want to blend in and go about their daily lives. The emotions attached to this attention are a constant roller coaster for the duration of one's stay. After I had been in Japan for more than two years, one night I was on the train from Fujisawa to Honmachi, a five-minute train trip from the main station to the station near my house. A college-aged woman, who had been staring at me for three of those five minutes, finally summoned up the courage to ask me in her perfect, textbook English, "Excuse me, do you have the time?" As I looked at the watch she was wearing, I politely replied telling her the time, patiently reminding myself that I was a representative of my country and continent. Mustering up the courage to say one sentence in English to this foreigner had likely been the bravest thing she'd ever done in her life.

I may be the only Canadian this woman ever has the chance to talk to. This simple two-sentence exchange, unnecessary as it was because her watch was certainly in working order, might be a highlight she talks to her grandchildren about one day. Even on my grumpy days or on the days when I wanted to be left alone, I reminded myself that for some, I may be the only chance they have to speak English outside of a classroom. I felt a duty to represent my culture with the same politeness and grace I constantly received from my host country.

I could have had it a lot worse. I am short enough to blend in to Japanese crowds, and as a brunette, I didn't stand out as starkly as blondes do. I did, however, find it amusing to have some students describe my hair colour as blonde. In a society where everyone has black hair, some didn't grasp the varying shades of brunette and therefore didn't have the words to describe my mousy hair.

Who I Am

In the almost three decades since I returned to Canada, I have often told people that I think everyone should live in another country for at least a year, especially one with a different first language and culture than their own. Travelling offers excellent opportunities to learn about new cultures, but there is no greater education of another culture and its people than being immersed in it for several months or years, whether for work or study. Going about one's daily life, having to struggle through linguistic and cultural differences, is a humbling experience and a great reminder that one culture is not necessarily better than another. There are different approaches to making and maintaining business and social relationships. There is more than one "right" way to shop in a department store. And whether you eat with your hands, chopsticks, or a fork, the main goal is to feed yourself—and if you fill your belly using any of these methods, you have been successful.

I knew almost nothing about Japanese culture before I left Canada in 1992. After three years, I certainly did not become an expert, but I did soak up fascinating information about its history, family structures, social interactions, and working relationships. I like to think that I also brought back to Canada a slightly higher level of respect and politeness in my work that I may not have developed had I not lived in The Land of Ultimate Politeness for three years.

During the time I worked in Japan, I helped people learn my language. Strengthening their English skills would give my students a leg up in their future jobs and open up new opportunities for them. My students often told me I was lucky to have been born in an English-speaking country, as I didn't have to learn English. To pursue better job opportunities, even in their own countries, many people around the world do need strong English skills. Realizing the impact that learning

English has on millions of non-native English speakers around the world impressed upon me that I AM lucky, and that I have a lot to offer to others in helping them creating their own opportunities.

But even when I was teaching, I realized I could learn just as much from my students as they could from me. I was thrilled and touched whenever my students wanted to share their culture with me.

More than anything, I learned about the wider world and myself in a way that I never would have had I never lived abroad. I was raised in a conservative Christian community and household. After living in Japan, I realized people who follow other religions, or none, had within them the same potential to be as good, generous, kind, selfish, cruel, open- or closed-minded, and funny as anyone else—regardless of cultural or religious influences or beliefs. I came back to Canada not so much rejecting the Christian values I was taught in my first eighteen years as embracing other religions. In essence, they are all similar in their base teachings: Be a good person, be good to yourself, and be kind to others.

I learned that I could maneuver through pretty much any situation and come through the other end. At times, that required relying on someone to translate for me, embarrassing myself, or having to fight through a massive misunderstanding—but I also learned how to communicate through a complete language barrier. All that's required is patience and a desire on the part of both sides to communicate with one another.

And I learned to laugh at myself. I've always had a good sense of humour, but as many of us do, I used to want to save face or come across as being more knowledgeable than I was. When you're standing in a department store, bogged down with items you need to pay for three floors above, you have no choice but to admit your lack of knowledge and retrace your steps to accomplish your goal. Those types of experiences all require a sense of humility and a willingness to adapt in ways that are not required in our own cultures.

My experiences in Japan taught me that there's no shame in having to admit, "I don't know." But from the moment you acknowledge what you don't know, you are immediately opened to the potential to learn. And for me, learning and growing is the exciting part of living in this big, culturally rich world.

ACKNOWLEDGEMENTS

First and foremost, deepest gratitude to **Andrea Idso**, my skilled and delightful editor, who has guided me through killing my wordiness and redundancies in three books now. Thank you for helping me tell the story of this, the most impactful period of my life. Here's to more collaboration in the future!

I owe a huge thank you to my former students, colleagues, and friends who were part of my life in Japan for more than three years. There are far too many to name, and unfortunately, I have long since lost touch with so many, but each one of my students, colleagues, and fellow expats brought something meaningful to my experience.

Keiko, thank you for generously taking me to the doctor in your Mercedes. The translation and moral support were hugely helpful in easing my fears!

Yukiko, your gift of the special doll your grandmother made, which I look at every day, still warms my heart all these years later. It's in a prominent spot in my bedroom!

Hirata-san, thank you for teaching me how to hold a golf club. Much gratitude, also, for leaving me with such warm memories of fun Saturday evenings spent at izakaya or karaoke. Even my mother forgave you for the squid guts because you are such a wonderful, kind man!

Toru, you were a great neighbour and a fun student. Thank you for helping me shop and trying, in solidarity, to eat an obscene amount of beef on my twenty-third birthday.

Akiko, thank you for also giving the beef-a-thon a shot. Thanks also to your family for taking me to other great beef restaurants knowing that I was missing my personal "national" cuisine.

Tomoko and your parents, thank you for being my Japanese family for three years. You welcomed me into your home so many times for visits and meals. Tomoko, your help with arranging train tickets and accommodation for travels throughout Japan was greatly appreciated. And thank you for being an excellent language teacher, helping my improve my Japanese skills for three years.

Stephen and **Brian**, thanks for the many belly laughs, and for being great travel companions … except for the puke … but that's become one of those "someday, we'll laugh about this" stories. And honestly, that's what made the Korea trip fun and memorable.

Beppu-sensei has sadly passed away since I left Japan. She was a wonderfully kind lady with a great sense of humour and a welcoming spirit. I will forever be grateful for her generous offering of weekly shamisen lessons and beef curry to Mark and me.

Ken, arigatō for being my grounding force from day one. One of the many lessons you taught me through our friendship and working relationship is one that I still cling to today. I was struggling with one of my lowest points of culture shock, and I was frustrated and angry with anyone and everyone. You said to me, "If you are having a problem with everyone around you, chances are you are the problem." You were right, and I still need to remind myself of that lesson from time to time.

To so many of my other students, thank you for taking me skiing, hiking, touring, eating, and karaoke singing. You each showed true Japanese hospitality and generosity while proudly teaching me your culture and traditions and asking about mine. Even now, I often emphasize that I learned as much from my students as they learned from me!

One of the long-lasting gifts that Japan gave me is a Christmas letter each year from my friend and former student **Naoto.** I have been back to Japan only twice since I left in 1995. Both times I looked up Naoto and arranged to meet him for coffee, which then turned into lunch and then an afternoon followed by dinner at his house with his family. Remember, Japanese people don't often entertain in their houses, so a wonderful sushi spread at his home with his wife, children, and parents was so special! And after dinner, we conversed long into the evening.

Naoto still lives halfway between Honmachi station and my former apartment building, and he's the same age as I am, so we were not only teacher and student, but also neighbours and remain good friends. Each year, when I receive the thick envelope with my address written in his handwriting, I save the letter for a time when I can sit down with a glass of wine and read it several times. Naoto is funny, intelligent, and philosophical, and he is one of my all-time favourite people to have a conversation with. Naoto, thank you for your friendship, your support of my time in Japan, and your kinship. We may not have seen each other for years, but I hear your deep, hearty laugh in my mind, and I miss our talks.

Although I only briefly mentioned **Canadian Teresa** toward the end of the book, she has been a constant in my life since that transitional period in the summer of 1995 when I returned to Japan to substitute teach. Instead of moving to Toronto or Vancouver, as I anticipated I would have to do to teach ESL in Canada, I ended up falling into my first of several great teaching jobs in Calgary. I found the job even before I completed my ESL diploma, so I have remained in or near our shared hometown all these years. When Teresa returned from Japan to Calgary, she lived here only briefly. Even though we have been far apart for the vast majority of our friendship, the camaraderie we established in Japan stands firm all these years later. Thank you, Teresa C., for your humour and presence in my life as a kind, wise friend who adds something meaningful to my life with every Facebook post or message.

Thank you, **Masayo and your mom**, for the treats from Japan. Whether it be a package of special green tea and Japanese snacks (Japan has the best snack foods!) or an in-person visit, it's always heartwarming to see or hear from you! I'm so proud of you, Masayo. It's been exciting to see you transform from a shy, giggly junior high school girl to a businesswoman who travels and lives a full and adventurous life! Thank you for your feedback on this book, making sure the cultural information was accurate. I look forward to handing you a signed copy in person!

I wish **my mom** and **Auntie Darlene** were still alive to see this book come to fruition. I knew my mom wasn't thrilled at the thought of my moving halfway across the world for a minimum of two years, but she was 100 per cent supportive in every way from the moment I told her about the job interview. She sent me goods from Canada when I needed or wanted something, and she dutifully trekked to the bank each month to deposit the money I sent home to pay off my student loan. And she kept my extended family up to speed on what I was doing and that, yes, I was surviving the earthquakes they were hearing about. Those weekly phone calls with my mom kept me connected to all that I couldn't experience at home while I was away. People's lives were going on, as was mine. Those phone calls, as well as letters from her, my sister, my grandma, and so many others, were the strings that connected me to my friends and family back home. The sound of a mother's voice is always comforting, regardless of the theme of the conversation. My mom always knew, as mothers do, when to send a package (even when I hadn't asked for one) and what to put in it.

Auntie Darlene was the reason I applied for the job in Japan. I would have never known about the opportunity had she not been scouring the *Calgary Herald* every Saturday in the summer of 1991, trying to help me find a job. Having her, my mom, and my sister come to visit at the two-year point of my stay was one of the highlights of my stint in Japan. I greatly miss my auntie, who passed away a few years ago. Thank you, Auntie, for always being supportive of me and for being a constant source of laughter in my life.

American Teresa, thank you for providing a homey place for us all to gather and to crash for the night on those karaoke, go-kart, or izakaya outings! Even though we have only seen each other once since we both left Japan, I'm glad we keep in close contact through Facebook and continue to laugh with each other from opposite sides of the 49th parallel. We will definitely make that long-overdue reunion happen one of these days. Just don't expect me to drink green beer!

And last, but most definitely not least, **Mark**. I will forever be grateful that we met and that we lived ten minutes from each other in Japan. Our mutual love of music, hiking, travel, and laughter has solidified a great friendship for thirty years and counting. I know we will both grow old laughing about some of our experiences in Japan, including fond memories of Beppu-sensei and her generous gift of free shamisen lessons and beef curry every Monday! I sincerely appreciate your feedback on this book, and I'm glad it brought back great memories for you, as well. Who could ask for a better beta reader than someone who not only points out your typos but also inserts funny personal comments about the memories on their manuscript pages? *Kanpai, tomodachi!*

ABOUT THE AUTHOR

Lorna Stuber has a B.Ed. with a double major in English Language Arts and Social Studies Education (University of Lethbridge), a Dip.Ed. in ESL Curriculum and Instruction (University of Calgary), and an Editing Certificate (Simon Fraser University). She spent her twenties teaching ESL in Japan and Calgary, Canada, and her thirties and forties teaching online high school English, Social Studies, and options for the Calgary Board of Education. After resigning from her latest teaching position, she began editing, writing, and ghostwriting as a freelancer. Lorna spends most of her money on plane tickets and accommodation in cool and often obscure travel destinations. She has now been to almost thirty countries on all continents except Antarctica, which is definitely on the list!

When she is not helping others fine-tune their writing, Lorna is snowshoeing, volunteering for local theatre, working on her own writing, and fulfilling her duties as the self-appointed "bad-influence auntie" to her friends' kids. She currently lives in Okotoks, Canada, with her dust elephants and her kitchen view of the Rocky Mountains.

Website: lornastuber.com

Facebook: facebook.com/lornastubereditor

LinkedIn: linkedin.com/in/lorna-stuber-freelance-editor-writer-ghostwriter

GLOSSARY OF JAPANESE TERMS AND PLACE NAMES

Aso

(proper noun) The name of both a city and a mountain on Japan's southern island. Mount Aso is Japan's largest active volcano. (Mount Fuji, the largest mountain in Japan, is technically classified as active, but it has not erupted in more than 300 years. Aso, on the other hand, is constantly spewing volcanic gasses and steam.)

basho

(noun) A grand sumo tournament. Basho run for two weeks and are held every January, March, May, July, September, and November. Their location rotates among Tōkyō (twice per year), Ōsaka (twice per year), Nagoya (once per year), and Fukuoka (once per year).

bentō

(noun) A takeout lunch box. Bentō boxes are usually divided into compartments to keep the different types of foods separate from each other.

bonito

(noun) A type of fish. Dried bonito flakes are a common topping on different types of Japanese foods, such as noodles dishes and okonomiyaki. They are also used in soups.

Chōgo

(proper noun) An area in the city of Fujisawa about forty-five kilometres west of central Tōkyō.

dōmo arigatō gozaimasu

(interjection) The most formal expression of thanks. *Thank you very much.*

Fujisawa

(proper noun) A city forty-five minutes west of central Tōkyō. In the early 1990s, the population of Fujisawa was roughly 300,000. Today, it is more than 430,000.

gaijin

(noun) A common Japanese term for *foreigner. Gai* means *outside; jin* means *person*.

gaikokujin

(noun) The more polite and more all-encompassing term for *foreigner. Gaijin* is usually used to refer to Caucasians or westerners, and *gaikokujin* is used for all foreigners. *Gaijin* is commonly used, but *gaikokujin* is considered more politically correct.

Gokurakuji

(proper noun) An area of Kamakura, Japan. Gokurakuji is also the name of both the Buddhist temple and train station in that part of Kamakura. There are several other temples throughout Japan with the name Gokurakuji.

gomi

(noun) Garbage, trash, waste.

hanabi

(noun) *Hana* means *flower* and *bi* means *fire*. Therefore, *Hanabi* literally means *fire flower* and is the word for fireworks. Hanabi in Japan are extravagant and make for popular outings on summer evenings.

Harajuku

(proper noun) A district in Tōkyō. Each area of Tōkyō has a distinct subculture or vibe, and Harajuku is known for pop culture; street performers; graffiti; and youthful, trendy fashion and shops, including cosplay.

hiragana

(noun) One of the three writing systems in the Japanese language. Hiragana is a script-style type of writing and is mainly used for Japanese words or syllables that do not have kanji attached to them, such as prepositions, adverbs, prefixes, suffixes, etc.

Hiratsuka

(proper noun) A small city of roughly 250,000 in Kanagawa prefecture, an hour west of Tōkyō by train and about fifteen minutes west of Fujisawa.

Hiroshima

(proper noun) Famed city on the south end of Honshū, Japan's main island. With a population of more than 1.1 million, Hiroshima is modern, as almost all of it was destroyed in the infamous atomic bombing during WW II. It is the site of the Hiroshima Peace Memorial Park and the Hiroshima Peace Memorial Museum, both of which commemorate the 1945 attack.

ippai

(adjective) *Full, much, a lot.* When someone is finished eating, *onaka-ga-ippai* is the full expression the person would use to indicate that they are full. *Onaka* means *stomach*.

izakaya

(noun) A casual bar serving snacks and drinks. Izakaya are popular for after-work social gatherings among colleagues for business people to entertain clients. Japanese people tend not to entertain in their homes nearly as much as Canadians and Americans do (mainly because homes are small, but also because Japanese people are more private than we westerners are). Izakaya offer fun, casual meeting places with plenty of food and drink options. The atmosphere is loud and fun.

Kanagawa

(proper noun) The Tōkyō-adjacent prefecture I lived in. (See *prefecture* further down in the glossary.) As it contains suburbs of Tōkyō, including Yokohama, Kanagawa is the second-most populous prefecture in Japan.

Kamakura

(proper noun) A small city located a forty-minute ride from my apartment by train or bicycle. Because of Kamakura's rich history as the former capital, it has become a main tourist attraction for Japanese and foreign travellers. It offers numerous shrines and temples; a beautiful coastline; multiple walking, biking, and hiking trails in the mountainous parts of the city; and the *Daibutsu*, the Great Buddha statue on the grounds of the Kōtokuin Temple. Kamakura's

Hachimangū Shrine—its most important Shinto shrine—can be reached by taking a 1.8 kilometre walk from the shore through torii gates. In the spring, this passage is wrapped by stunning cherry blossom trees in bloom.

kana

(noun) The syllable-based writing system in Japanese. There are two types of kana: hiragana is used mainly for prepositions, adverbs, prefixes, and suffixes; katakana is used for foreign words.

kanji

(noun) The Chinese characters used in Japanese writing. Kanji are used to represent nouns, adjectives, adverbs, and verbs. These are the same characters used in China, so anyone who can read kanji will be able to read in Japan, China, Taiwan, Singapore, and anywhere else that Chinese characters are used in writing. Pronunciation between the languages differs, but the meaning represented by kanji is the same across cultures. In Japanese, kanji are interspersed with or preceded by hiragana to create the full Japanese word.

kanpai

(interjection) *Cheers!* An evening at an izakaya or karaoke box officially begins when all attendees have a drink in hand and can raise their glasses together to offer a toast. The literal translation is *empty the glass!* It is considered rude to drink from one's glass before everyone has a beverage and the toast has been made.

karaoke

(noun) A popular form of entertainment in Japan, karaoke is different there than in Canada. Friends, colleagues, business people, and clients will gather and go to a karaoke studio, where they can rent a private room by the hour and sing together. Karaoke studios offer room service for drinks and food.

katakana

(noun) One of three written Japanese alphabets or scripts. Katakana is used for words from foreign languages that are used in Japanese. For example, coffee is pronounced kōhi in Japanese and written in katakana as コーヒー.

kin

(noun) Gold, money.

Kinkaku-ji

(proper noun) The famed Gold Pavilion or gold temple in Kyōto, Japan. A Zen Buddhist temple covered in gold leaf, Kinkaku-ji is one of the most well-recognized and frequently-visited buildings in Japan.

Kinokuniya

(proper noun) A chain of international bookstores. There are Kinokuniya stores throughout Japan offering a great selection of books in English and other languages. When I lived there, the closest Kinokuniya to me was in Yokohama, about twenty minutes away by train, so I frequently shopped there since this was before the days of the Internet.

kotatsu

(noun) A Japanese-style coffee table. Usually, kotatsu are roughly knee-height and contain a heater underneath the removable tabletop. Once the top is removed, a blanket is placed over the frame of the kotatsu and extends eighteen to twenty-four inches beyond the frame. When the top is placed back on and the heater is turned on, people can sit at the kotatsu with the blanket on their legs, thereby keeping the heat in. Kotatsu are used to keep oneself warm while drinking tea or eating in the winter in lieu of central heating, which Japan does not have.

Kyōto

(proper noun) A former capital of Japan. Kyōto is considered the best place in Japan to see traditional Japan all in one city. It is home to the iconic Kinkaku-ji (the Gold Pavilion) as well as several festivals and additional temples and shrines. The Gion district in Kyōto is a visitor's best chance at seeing traditionally attired geisha walking through the streets.

mawashi

(noun) The loincloth sumo wrestlers wear when training and competing.

mikan

(noun) The Japanese word for tangerine-sized oranges—those little oranges that we all love. I grew up knowing them as *Christmas oranges* because we could only get them around Christmastime, which is when they are in season. Of course, the fresh mikan in Japan are even more delicious than the ones we get in the supermarkets in Canada.

miso

(noun) A Japanese seasoning made from fermented soybeans and sometimes from rice, seaweed, and barley. Miso serves as the base for miso soup, which accompanies many Japanese meals. It can also be used as a seasoning for salads and other dishes.

murasaki

(adjective) Purple.

Nagano

(proper noun) The capital city of Nagano prefecture, about three hours northwest of Tōkyō by train. Nagano is situated in the Japan Alps and is famous for hosting the 1998 Winter Olympics.

Nagasaki

(proper noun) A city of slightly more than 400,000 near Hiroshima, Nagasaki was also attacked in WW II with an atomic bomb. As a major port city on Japan's southern island and easily accessible by sea to South Korea and mainland China, Nagasaki has an extensive history of trade and missionary settlement.

nandarō

(interjection) A somewhat crass way of saying "What?" as in "What the hell…?" Usually used by men.

natsukashii

(adjective) The feeling of nostalgia, but deeper than that. A longing and a fondness for something meaningful and heartwarming from the past. It encompasses joy and gratitude for an experience that you know you will never have again.

ne

(interjection) An expression used in seeking affirmation, such as "right?" or "isn't that so?" Our Canadian equivalent is "eh?" For example, when we say, "Nice weather, eh?", the *eh* functions the same way as *ne* does in Japanese. An appropriate response would be "*Sou, da ne*!" ("Yeah, that's right!") or "*Sou desu yo*!" ("I agree!")

Obon

(proper noun) Festival of the Souls, the three-day-long Buddhist celebration honouring the souls of one's ancestors. Obon takes place in August and is a time when family members hang lanterns outside their homes to welcome the souls of their ancestors. Rituals include performing special dances, making and eating specific foods, and visiting graves with food and flowers. Obon is one of the three major holiday seasons in Japan, the others being Golden Week and New Year.

okonomiyaki

(noun) Japanese pancake. The batter is made with flour and eggs, and base ingredients include cabbage and usually a protein such as pork or shrimp. Toppings and other fillings can include a fried egg, other vegetables, seaweed flakes, okonomi-sauce, and mayonnaise.

Ōsaka

(proper noun) A large, fairly modern city minutes from Kyōto, Ōsaka is home to a beautiful castle surrounded by a moat as well as cherry blossom and plum trees.

prefecture

(noun) A regional district with its own local government, similar to a province or state.

rōma-ji

(noun) The word referring to the Roman or "English" alphabet. Most written Japanese uses kana or kanji, but sometimes it uses rōma-ji, or Roman lettering, particularly in marketing and advertising.

-san

(noun, honorific) The honorific used at the end of someone's last name, *-san* is used for adult men and women, married or not, as the all-inclusive equivalent to Mr., Mrs., Ms., or Miss. For example, use *Tanaka-san* to politely address someone named Keiko Tanaka. First names only are not traditionally used to address people but to do so in informal settings or between friends is becoming more common.

sayōnara

(interjection) Goodbye. *Sayōnara* is usually a more formal or more final goodbye. When saying "good night" or "see you later" to friends or colleagues, one would instead say *otsukaresame-deshita.*

seiza

(noun) Traditional Japanese seated position with the front of your lower legs flat on the ground and your bottom resting on your heels. Most foreigners sitting seiza for the first few times find their legs and feet falling asleep within a few minutes, but with practice, one can comfortably maintain seiza position for more than thirty minutes.

sensei

(noun, honorific) In English, *sensei* translates to *teacher*. Sensei means master and is used not only for schoolteachers but for anyone who is a master of a certain skill, such as martial arts, flower arrangement, or other arts. *Sensei* is also used to address doctors, lawyers, etc., as a term of high respect for people in those roles. It is used in place of *-san* for people in these roles. For example, someone whose family name is

Tanaka would be addressed as *Tanaka-san* in everyday use, but if this person were a doctor, they would be addressed as *Tanaka-sensei*.

Shinjuku

(proper noun) A ward or district in Tōkyō that is home to the biggest and busiest railway station in the world and is therefore a hub for travel and business.

shinkansen

(noun) Japan's famous bullet train. Shinkansen are comfortable, clean, efficient, and—of course—speedy. They serve as one of the best ways to travel throughout the country.

shiokara

(noun) Fermented, salted squid, including the intestines. I cannot attest to the taste of this, as this is where I drew one of my culinary lines, but according to my mother, it's "not very good." An acquired taste, I presume.

shōji

(noun) *Shōji* is used to refer to screens, doors, and windows with the traditional lattice design of wood frames with paper panes. Shōji is also the word for the paper used in the panes. Made of wood fibers, the white shōji paper is bendable but thick.

tatami

(noun) The large traditional mats used for flooring in Japan. Tatami were traditionally made from rice straw but these days may also be made of wood chips or synthetic materials.

Tateshina

(proper noun) The name of both a town and a mountain in Nagano prefecture.

Tōkyō

(proper noun) A busy and densely populated city. I often compare New York to Tōkyō in that they are both culturally diverse, vibrant, exciting, jam-packed with arts and culture, and easy to get around using the efficient train and subway systems. Like New York, Tōkyō has several distinct wards, each with its own vibe and subculture.

tomodachi

(noun) Friend

tonkatsu

(noun) Deep-fried pork cutlet, often served with shredded cabbage, plain white rice, pickles, and miso soup.

unadon

(noun) A dish of grilled eel served on top of a bowl of rice and topped with unagi sauce, which is a barbecue or teriyaki-type sauce especially suited for the eel.

unagi

(noun) Freshwater eel, a popular food in Japan. It's delicious and healthy—a great source of several vitamins, omega-3, and protein.

Unchi-kun

(proper noun) Mr. Poop! The smiling, bright-eyed little poop emoji that we see on our cellphones and social media these days. Unchi-kun was wildly popular in Japan at least two decades before he migrated to Canada and the US.

wan wan

(interjection) The Japanese phrase for the sound that dogs make, equivalent to the English woof woof.

yabusame

(noun) A throwback to the days of samurai, yabusame is a spectacular display of archery on horseback. Archers wear full samurai gear and shoot at targets while racing a horse at full speed down a dirt track.

Yamato

(proper noun) A small city half an hour north of Fujisawa's main train station. Yamato is smaller than Fujisawa, with a population of slightly more than 230,000. Yamato's main train station is one of the access points to Tōkyō from Kanagawa prefecture. Yamato city is where Ken, my American co-worker and friend, lived.

zaisu

(noun) A legless chair that sits on the ground. Zaisu are often, but not always, used for sitting at a kotatsu.

Zengyō

(proper noun) The second station north of Fujisawa's main train station, after Honmachi. Zengyō is the closest train stop to where my friend Mark lived.